The Crusades
Almanac

The Crusades
Almanac

Written by Michael J. O'Neal
Edited by Marcia Merryman Means and Neil Schlager

U·X·L

An imprint of Thomson Gale, a part of The Thomson Corporation

THOMSON

GALE

Detroit • New York • San Francisco • San Diego • New Haven, Conn. • Waterville, Maine • London • Munich

THOMSON

GALE

The Crusades: Almanac

Written by Michael J. O'Neal

Edited by Marcia Merryman Means and Neil Schlager

Project Editor
Julie L. Carnagie

Permissions
Lori Hines, Susan J. Rudolph,
William A. Sampson

Imaging and Multimedia
Lezlie Light, Mike Logusz, Kelly A. Quin

Product Design
Pamela Galbreath, Jennifer Wahi

Composition
Evi Seoud

Manufacturing
Rita Wimberley

LIBRARY OF CONGRESS CATALOGING-IN-PUBLICATION DATA

O'Neal, Michael J., 1949-

The Crusades: Almanac / written by Michael J. O'Neal ; edited by Marcia Merryman Means and Neil Schlager.

p. cm. – (The Crusades reference library)

Includes bibliographical references and index.

ISBN 0-7876-9176-3 (alk. paper)

1. Crusades–Juvenile literature. I. Means, Marcia Merryman. II. Schlager, Neil, 1966-

III. Title. IV. Series.

D157.O34 2004
909.07–dc22 2004018003

Contents

Reader's Guide

The term "crusade" is commonly used today to refer to a dedicated, enthusiastic effort. It usually means a total, all-out attempt to correct a problem, such as combating drunk driving or saving an endangered species from extinction. When people use the word "crusade," though, they may not recognize its distinctly religious meaning and history, even though they might embark on their crusade with religious enthusiasm.

The "Crusades" (with a capital "C") were a series of military campaigns launched by the Christian countries of western Europe in the late eleventh century. During these battles tens of thousands of people went to war in the Middle East. Their goal was to recapture the Holy Land, or Palestine, from the Muslims and restore it to Christian control. The focus of the Crusaders was the holy city of Jerusalem, now part of the Jewish nation of Israel on the eastern shore of the Mediterranean Sea and still a holy site to three religions: Judaism, Islam, and Christianity. But the impact of the Crusades was felt throughout that region of the world and in Europe.

The First Crusade was launched in late 1095 and ended with the capture of Jerusalem in 1099. The last

Crusade took place in the late 1200s. Historians identify seven separate Crusades, although there were two other highly irregular Crusades that are not generally numbered. The exact number is not important, for the Crusades were a single extended conflict that was fought over the course of two centuries. As the military and diplomatic situation in Jerusalem and the surrounding areas changed, successive waves of European troops flowed into the region to capture a key city or to expel an opposing army that had recaptured the same city. Each of these waves represented one of the Crusades. After each Crusade, particularly the early ones, some of the European invaders remained in the Middle East to rule over Christian kingdoms they had established. Many others returned to their homelands. During the periods between each Crusade, there was relative peace between the warring parties, although tensions simmered beneath the surface.

The Muslim world was slow to respond to the Crusaders. For many decades Muslims were too busy fighting among themselves for power and influence in the Middle East and lands beyond to recognize the threat that the Crusaders posed. Only after they mounted organized resistance were they able to drive the Crusaders out of the Middle East. Hundreds of years later, many Muslims continue to regard westerners as "crusaders" bent on occupying their holy territory.

Historians continue to debate whether, from a European Christian perspective, the Crusades were a success. While the first ended successfully with the capture of Jerusalem, some of the later Crusades were military and political disasters, at least from the point of view of the Europeans. All historians agree, though, that the Crusades would have a profound effect on the development of European civilization. They opened trade routes and promoted commerce, they led to never-before-seen exploration and cultural contact, and they provided inspiration for poets and novelists. They also laid the groundwork for conflict and religious strife that continues in the twenty-first century.

Features and Format

The Crusades: Almanac covers the Crusades in thirteen thematic chapters, each examining an element of the two-hundred-year time period. The volume takes the reader through many aspects of this lengthy conflict. Included are chapters on the origins, history, and aftermath of the Crusades and on the holy city of Jerusalem and the land of Palestine as the focal site of three faiths. There are also profiles of the various groups of Muslims and Christians involved in the fight and descriptions of knights and the conduct of warfare. More than fifty black-and-white images illustrate the text. Numerous sidebars highlight interesting people and fascinating facts connected with the Crusades. The volume includes a glossary, a timeline, words to know, research and activity ideas, sources for further reading, and a subject index.

The Crusades Reference Library

The Crusades: Almanac is only one component of a three-part U•X•L Crusades Reference Library. The set also includes one volume of biographies and another of primary source documents:

- *The Crusades: Biographies* presents the biographies of twenty-five men and women who lived at the time of the Crusades and experienced the battles or the effects of these wars. Profiled are famous figures, such as Richard the Lionheart, king of England; the Muslim warrior Saladin, and Saint Francis of Assisi, as well as lesser-known people, among them, the sultana of Egypt Shajarat al-Durr and the Arab soldier and writer Usamah ibn Munqidh.

- *The Crusades: Primary Sources* offers twenty-four full or excerpted documents, speeches, and literary works from the Crusades era. Included are "political" statements, such as Pope Urban II's speech calling for the First Crusade. There are also accounts of battles and sieges as well as other events, such as the slaughter of Jews in Europe by Crusaders on their way to the Holy Land. Included are samplings from literature, among them, excerpts from the epic poem *The Song of Roland* and a chapter of the Koran. The Arabic view of the times are featured in such writings as a Muslim historian's view of the Mongol invasions. The Byzantine perspective is seen, for example, in portions of *The Alexiad,* a biography of the emperor Alexius I Comnenus by his daughter.

- A cumulative index of all three titles in The Crusades Reference Library is also available.

Acknowledgments

Several people deserve our gratitude for their assistance with this project. We are indebted to everyone at U•X•L and Thomson Gale who assisted with the production, particularly Julie Carnagie, who provided help at all stages; we also thank Carol Nagel for her support.

Marcia Merryman Means

Neil Schlager

About the Author

Michael J. O'Neal received a B.A. and a Ph.D. in English and Linguistics from Bowling Green State University in Ohio. After teaching at the college level for a decade, he became a freelance writer and book editor. This is his seventh book for younger readers. He lives in Idaho, where he enjoys horseback riding in the company of his wife and their two dogs.

About the Editors

Marcia Merryman Means and Neil Schlager are managing editor and president, respectively, of Schlager Group Inc., an editorial services company with offices in Florida and Vermont. Schlager Group publications have won numerous honors, including four RUSA awards from the American Library Association, two Reference Books Bulletin/Booklist Editors' Choice awards, two New York Public Library Outstanding Reference awards, and two *CHOICE* awards.

Comments and Suggestions

We welcome your comments on *The Crusades: Almanac* and suggestions for other topics in history to consider. Please write to Editors, *The Crusades: Almanac,* U•X•L, 27500 Drake Road, Farmington Hills, Michigan 48331-3535; call toll-free 800-877-4253; send faxes to 248-699-8097; or send e-mail via http://www.galegroup.com.

Timeline of Events

Tenth century B.C.E. The Jewish Temple of Solomon is constructed in Jerusalem.

63 B.C.E. Jerusalem falls under the control of the Roman Empire.

70 C.E. Romans destroy the Second Temple of Solomon in Jerusalem.

313 Roman Emperor Constantine converts to Christianity.

Fifth century The breakup of the Roman Empire creates the Byzantine Empire in the East; Jerusalem falls into the hands of the Byzantines.

c. 610 Muhammad experiences revelations that lead to the founding of Islam.

632 The death of Muhammad marks the beginning of a long period of Islamic civil war and separation of Islam into Sunni and Shiite sects.

638 The second Muslim caliph, Umar, captures the city of Jerusalem.

1054 The Great Schism divides the Christian church into two branches: the Roman Catholic Church in the West and the Eastern, or Greek, Orthodox Church in the East.

1071 Seljuk Turks seize control of Jerusalem; The Byzantine Empire is defeated by the Seljuks at the Battle of Manzikert.

November 27, 1095 Pope Urban II preaches a sermon at Clermont, France, announcing the Crusades.

1095–99 The First Crusade is waged ending successfully with the capture of Jerusalem.

1144 The city of Edessa falls to Imad al-Din Zengi.

March 31, 1146 Bernard of Clairvaux preaches the Second Crusade.

1148 Under Louis VII, the Crusader army is defeated at Damascus, ending the Second Crusade.

1153 The city of Ascalon falls to the Crusaders under Baldwin; the last major victory of the Crusaders.

October 2, 1187 Jerusalem falls to Saladin.

1189 Frederick Barbarossa departs for the Holy Land, launching the Third Crusade.

1191 Richard the Lionheart of England and Philip of France arrive in the Holy Land.

1192–93 Richard and Saladin conclude the terms of a truce ending the Third Crusade.

1193 Saladin dies.

1199 Pope Innocent III calls the Fourth Crusade.

June 1202 The Fourth Crusade departs for Venice, Italy.

1203 The Fourth Crusade departs Venice for Constantinople.

April 1204 Constantinople is sacked.

May 1204 Crusaders leave Constantinople.

1212 The Children's Crusade is launched.

1218 The Fifth Crusade arrives in the Holy Land.

1218–19 Damietta, in Egypt, is besieged.

July 24, 1221 The Fifth Crusade, south of Damietta, is defeated.

September 8, 1221 The Crusaders return to Europe.

August 1227 Frederick II departs on the Sixth Crusade.

February 28, 1229 Frederick II and al-Malik sign the Treaty of Jaffa, restoring Jerusalem to the Christians and ending the Sixth Crusade.

1244 The Khwarismians overrun Jerusalem.

1248 King Louis IX leaves Europe for the Seventh Crusade.

1249 King Louis IX arrives in the Middle East and captures Damietta in Egypt.

1250 King Louis IX's forces are defeated by the Egyptians, ending the Seventh Crusade.

1258 Mongols capture Baghdad.

1260 Baybars defeats the Muslims at the Battle of Ain Jalut.

May 18, 1291 The city of Acre falls.

Words to Know

A

Allah: The name of the deity in the Islamic faith.

B

Byzantine Empire: The eastern half of the Roman Empire, whose capital was Byzantium, renamed Constantinople.

C

Caliph: Any successors to Muhammad, the founder of Islam, and the spiritual and earthly leader of Islam.

Caliphate: The office of a caliph or the territory ruled by a caliph.

Catapult: A large sling used to hurl firebombs and anything else that could cause harm over the walls of a fortified castle or city.

Cathars: A sect, or subgroup, of Christians that appeared in southern France around the time of the Fifth Crusade and who were declared heretics, or people who disagreed with established church beliefs, by the pope and persecuted.

Chanson de Geste: A "song of deeds," a form of heroic literature in medieval France.

Chivalry: From the French word *chevalerie,* meaning "skill in handling a horse," a code of ethics, or moral values, and behavior expected of all knights, especially those who took part in the Crusades.

Crusades: The military expeditions launched from the late eleventh through the thirteenth centuries by Christian European countries to reclaim the Holy Lands of the Middle East.

E

Emir: A ruler, chief, or commander in an Islamic country or region.

F

Fatimids: The name of the Egyptian Shiite Muslim dynasty that ruled Jerusalem.

Feudalism: The social and economic system that existed in Europe during the Middle Ages; refers primarily to the shared duties of noble landowners, the peasants who worked on their estates, and the knights who protected them.

Franj: The Muslim word for Latin Christians, derived from the word "Frank" because large numbers of the Crusaders were Frankish, or French.

Franjistan: The Muslim term for the homeland of the Franj, or the Franks.

Frank: Term often used to refer generally to the Crusaders, whatever their national origin, because many were from the Frankish empire, or France.

G

Genocide: The mass slaughter of a religious, national, racial, or ethnic group.

Great Schism: The 1054 breakup of the Christian church into the Roman Catholic Church in the West and the Eastern Orthodox Church in the East.

H

Holocaust: The name usually given to the mass slaughter of Jews by the German Nazis before and during World War II (1939–45); used often to refer to any genocide.

Holy Land: Palestine, largely modern-day Israel; from a European Christian perspective, the sites of events in the life of Jesus Christ, including the Holy Sepulchre, or Christ's tomb.

I

Islam: Founded in the seventh century by Muhammad, the religion practiced by Muslims and the dominant religion of the Middle East; means "submission" to the will of Allah, or God. In older texts, often called "Muhammadanism," but this word is considered offensive by Muslims.

K

Knight: From the Anglo-Saxon word *cniht,* meaning "boy," a young man-at-arms who owed allegiance to his feudal lord.

Koran: Often spelled Qur'an, the sacred scripture, or holy book, of the Islamic faith.

L

Levant: From the French word *lever,* meaning "to rise" (referring to the rising of the Sun in the East), a term that indicates the countries around the eastern Mediterranean Sea.

M

Mamluks: The rulers of Egypt at the end of the Crusades.

Medieval: Term used for the Middle Ages.

Middle Ages: The period of European history from about 500, when the Roman Empire collapsed, to about 1500; sometimes called the Dark Ages.

Minnesängers (MINN-uh-seng-erz): German poet-singers of the Middle Ages who sang of courtly love.

Mongols: A nomadic tribe from Asia that overran much of the Middle East during the thirteenth century.

Muslim: A member of the Islamic faith.

N

Normans: People from Normandy, a region in France; often used to refer to all French knights during the Crusades.

O

Outremer (oo-tre-MARE): French term, meaning "the land overseas," for the Latin Christian colonies established after the First Crusade.

P

Patriarch: A high-ranking cleric, or clergyman, of the Eastern Orthodox Church.

R

Regent: A person who rules a kingdom on behalf of a monarch who is disabled, absent, or, as was usually the case, a child.

Relic: Any object associated with Jesus Christ or with one of the saints, most important among them being pieces of the cross on which Christ was crucified.

S

Saracen: European word for Muslims during the Crusades; a term probably derived from the Arabic *Sharkeyn,* meaning "eastern peoples."

Seljuk: A large, warlike clan of Turks that overran much of the Byzantine Empire and seized control of Jerusalem in 1071.

Shiite: A sect, or subgroup, of Islam that disagrees with the mainstream Muslims.

Siege: A military tactic of surrounding a fortified town or castle with the goal of cutting it off from outside aid and, over time, starving the inhabitants into surrender.

Sultan: An Arabic ruler, usually of a local region called a sultanate.

Sunni: The major sect, or subgroup, of the Islamic faith.

T

Troubadours: Poet-singers of medieval Europe, especially southern France, northern Italy, and northern Spain.

***Trouvères* (Troo-VAIR):** Poet-singers of northern medieval France.

V

Vassal: A feudal tenant of a lord.

Research and Activity Ideas

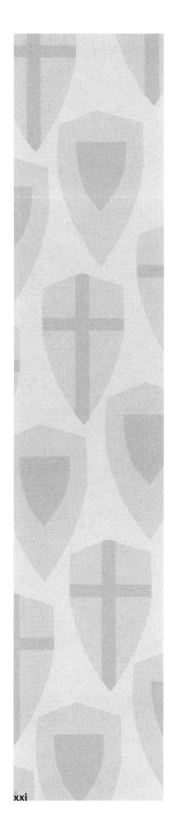

The following research and activity ideas are intended to offer suggestions for complementing social studies and history curricula; to trigger additional ideas for enhancing learning; and to provide cross-disciplinary projects for library and classroom use.

Building a Model: Conduct further research about an event during the Crusades, such as a particular battle or siege. An example might be the siege of Antioch during the First Crusade or the siege of Acre in 1291. Then build a scale model that would show the city, the arrangement of the troops on both sides, and other significant events during the battle or siege. Another possibility is to conduct further research into the architecture of castles during the Middle Ages and build a scale model of a castle that might have been found in the Middle East at the time of the Crusades. Or you might build a model of a siege engine that was used to hurl missiles at castles and fortified cities during the Crusades. Be prepared to explain to your classmates how the siege engine works.

Maps: Frequently, the course of a battle during the Crusades turned on characteristics of the geography of the place where the battle was fought. For example, a force of soldiers might have had to travel through a narrow mountain pass, where they met the danger of ambush, or surprise attack, by opposing forces. In the desert climate of the Middle East, Crusaders often faced great hardship because of the heat and lack of water, so they took different routes to their objective that would take them over cooler mountain passes. Conduct research on this aspect of the Crusades and develop a map showing the Crusaders' route during a particular battle campaign. Pretend that you are one of the military commanders planning the movement of your forces and draw the map that you would give to your troops.

Poetry: Imagine that you are an eyewitness to one of the key events of the Crusades. Examples might be the siege of Antioch or the capture of Jerusalem during the First Crusade or one of the battles between Richard I and Saladin. Write a poem that expresses how the event might have appeared to you. You might read some examples of *chansons de geste,* or "songs of deeds," and attempt to write your poem in language that sounds like it might have been used in such a poem. Or imagine that you are one of the Crusaders or a Muslim fighter. Write a letter home, describing the event to your family or perhaps to a noble in Europe or a Muslim religious leader.

What If … ?: Historians like to imagine what might have happened if events had taken a different course. Picture how the world might be different today if the Crusades had not taken place. Or imagine that a specific event of the Crusades had turned out differently. For example, what would have happened if Tancred had not found the large wooden timbers that the Crusaders used to build towers to get over the walls of Jerusalem in 1099? (Remember that an Egyptian army was on its way to help defend the city but did not arrive in time.) Write a short paper in which you consider how things might have turned out differently.

How Do Historians Know?: The events of the Crusades took place between about seven hundred and nine hundred years ago. Participants did not keep the kinds of accurate records that might be kept today, and there were no journalists who covered the Crusades on a day-to-basis. How do historians today know what really happened? What documents do they rely on? Conduct research into these questions. Compile a list of sources that historians use. Examples might include the accounts of William of Tyre, an archbishop and historian who lived in the Holy Land; Raymond of Agiles, a French chronicler of the Crusades; or Anna Comnena, the daughter of the Byzantine emperor at the time of the First Crusade.

Politics: Many of the events of the Crusades were influenced by politics. The kingdoms that the Crusaders established in the Middle East were no different from any other kingdoms at the time. People competed for power, influence, territory, and money. There were many arguments over who would rule particular cities, including Jerusalem. In many cases, queens played a central role. Although at that time a queen could not rule by herself, the man she married would become king, so marriages were often political arrangements. Muslims, too, dealt with political infighting, or fighting between different but related groups, and were not always unified in their response to the Crusades. Conduct research into this aspect of the Crusades and write a short paper about the influence of politics on events.

The Art of War: Imagine that you are a "photojournalist" sent to cover the Crusades. Of course, the camera had not yet been invented, so you have to record your impressions in sketches and drawings. Create a series of such drawings for a particular event during the Crusades. What would your drawings emphasize? Would they try to persuade your viewers back in Europe that the Crusaders were noble and brave? Or would they focus on the brutality and violence of the Crusades? Or imagine that you were sent by one of the popes or by a European or Islamic ruler to "cover" a Crusade. Write the report that you would send home. Would your report be an honest account of the events that took place? Or would you think it necessary to tell the person to whom you are writing what you think he or she wants to hear?

Book Report: Many books have been written about the Crusades. Some study the Crusades as a whole, others focus on one of the Crusades, and still others look at an aspect of the Crusades, such their impact on Jewish people the part played by women, or the role of knightly orders, such as the Knights Templars and the Knights Hospitallers. Go to your library and find such a book that interests you. Write a report that you can share with your classmates. What did you learn about the Crusades that you did not know? Or read a novel or other work of literature that has a Crusade setting. An example might be Sir Walter Scott's novel *The Talisman.* How does the author use events of the Crusades in the work of literature?

History from the Bottom Up: Much of history, as it is studied at present, focuses on events from the perspective of kings, popes, generals, and the nobility. This view of history, from the top down, looks at the broad sweep of events. Another approach to history, though, is to look at it from the viewpoint of people who are not famous: common foot soldiers, people along the route that the Crusaders followed to the Holy Land (including European Jews), servants and laborers (for example, washerwomen or blacksmiths) who accompanied the crusading armies, wives who went on Crusade with their husbands, and the like. Write an account of one of the Crusades, or one event during the Crusades, from this "bottom-up" perspective.

The Crusades on the World Wide Web: The Internet contains many sites devoted to the Crusades or some aspect of the Crusades. Conduct Internet research on a topic that interests you and write a student guide to Crusade resources on the Web. You might focus on one topic, for example, sites devoted to the Knights Templars or those devoted to studies of the Crusades from an Islamic perspective. Or create a "virtual museum," that is, an online museum, of sites that contain images associated with the Crusades: Jerusalem (including sights that pilgrims might have visited), Crusader castles, Islamic-influenced buildings that still survive in Spain, and weapons and other objects that might be found in a real museum. Write a "museum guide" that would conduct viewers through these Internet sites.

Biographies: Many of the historical figures who took part in the Crusades were interesting and colorful figures. Examples include King Richard I of England, Frederick II of the Holy Roman Empire, and the Muslim general Saladin. Conduct research into the life of one of these figures and write a brief report. Or you might research the life of an important background figure, such as one of the popes who called a Crusade (for example, Urban II or Innocent III). What impact did this person have on the Crusades? What impact did the Crusades have on this person's life?

The Reconciliation Walk: On July 15, 1999, the nine hundredth anniversary of the capture of Jerusalem during the First Crusade, a Reconciliation Walk was held in the city. The goal of this walk was to try to acknowledge the mistakes of the Crusades and bring Christians, Muslims, and Jews together. Conduct research into the Reconciliation Walk. Who led the effort? Describe the event. Do you think such an event accomplished its goal? Write a brief report and share it with your classmates.

Geographical Worlds
at the Time of the Crusades

One thousand years ago the nations and peoples of Europe, western Asia, and the Middle East held differing cultural and religious beliefs. For hundreds of years tensions and conflicts had divided these clusters of nations. Tensions eventually came to a boiling point in November 1095, when the pope of the Catholic Church, Urban II, called for a Crusade to the Middle Eastern nation of Palestine to reclaim for Christianity the holy city of Jerusalem.

The nations and peoples of Europe, western Asia, and the Middle East

A full understanding of the Crusades requires an understanding of these different cultural groups. Each had its own history, and all shared an interest in the holy places in and around Jerusalem. The groups that would play a role in the Crusades were the Europeans, the peoples of the Byzantine Empire, the followers of the religion of Islam, and the Jews.

Europe in 1095

Despite their many differences, the countries of Europe, also known as the "West," shared a belief in Christianity. The version of Christianity that dominated Europe was that of the Catholic Church, centered in Rome. The leader of the Christian church was the pope, who often wielded more power than the kings of Europe, or at least tried to. Because the peoples of Europe spoke so many different languages, the Christian church conducted its affairs in Latin. Latin was the language of the old Roman Empire that had ruled these nations for centuries. It thus became the common language not only of Christian priests, monks, and bishops but also of nearly all educated people in Europe, who generally received their education through the church. Accordingly, this group of European countries was often referred to as "Latin Christendom." It included such nations as England, Scotland, Ireland, France, Germany, Italy, and northern Spain as well as the countries of Scandinavia and the "Low Countries," such as Holland.

The Byzantine Empire

A second major cultural-religious center was the Byzantine Empire. This empire was formed out of the remains of the Roman Empire in the East. The name comes from the empire's ancient capital city, Byzantium, although the city's name was later changed to Constantinople (present-day Istanbul, in Turkey). Because it was more unified, this empire, which stretched from portions of Italy through southeastern Europe and into western Asia, was more powerful than the separate and often quarrelsome nations of the West.

Like the West, the Byzantine Empire was Christian, although the version of Christianity practiced in this region was called Eastern Orthodox or, frequently, Greek Orthodox. The primary language of the church was Greek, but many other languages were used locally. Unlike the nations of the West, which fell into a period of backwardness and turmoil with the end of the Roman Empire, the East developed a rich and complex culture and amassed a great deal of wealth.

Islam

A third major cultural group formed around the religion called Islam, members of which are called Muslims. In

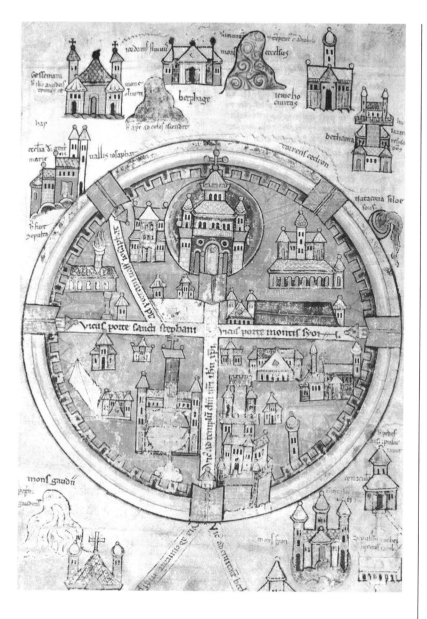

A manuscript illumination from Robert the Monk's "Chronicle of the Crusades" showing a medieval map of the city of Jerusalem. Jerusalem is considered a holy city for the Jews, the Christians, and the Muslims. *©Gianni Dagli Orti/Corbis. Reproduced by permission.*

1095 Islam was the dominant religion in the countries of the Middle East as well as in parts of Asia. (Europeans called this region the Middle East to distinguish it from the countries of Asia, which were farther away and therefore called the Far East.) The Middle East extends roughly from northeastern Africa through the Arabian Peninsula and into western Asia. At the time of the Crusades it included such countries as Persia, Syria, Palestine, and Egypt.

From its beginnings in the seventh century, the Islamic world expanded from its roots in the city of Mecca (in today's Saudi Arabia) to include much of North Africa, Arabia, western Asia, and even parts of Europe. Also converting to Islam were the peoples of central Asia, whom the Byzantines referred to as Turks. The Turks in time became powerful militarily, and eventually they overran many of the other Muslim nations, including Syria and Persia.

The Jews

A final group that played a role in the Crusades was the Jews. Unlike Muslims and Christians (both Latin Christians and Eastern Orthodox Christians), the Jews did not have a homeland in any specific country or group of countries. They were widely spread throughout all three regions and preserved their cultural identity through ancient religious practices and a common language, Hebrew. Because they often remained separate from the cultures surrounding them, and because those cultures saw them as different, Jews were often subjected to harsh persecution (prejudice), particularly in the West.

Claimants to the Holy Land

The historical journey that these cultural and religious groups followed and that eventually brought them into conflict before and during the Crusades was long and complex. It started during the early history of Judaism and continued through the first centuries of the Christian era.

Judaism

From a historical perspective, the first seeds of the Crusades were sown as far back as the tenth century B.C.E. (Before the Common Era). At that time the Israelites, or the Jews, under the leadership of the Old Testament king Solomon, constructed a magnificent temple (a place of worship for Jews) in the city of Jerusalem. In a room called the Holy of Holies, the temple housed the Ark of the Covenant. The ark contained the tablets on which the Ten Commandments, delivered to the Old Testament prophet Moses, were carved. Within the temple was a bare rock called the Foundation Stone. According to the Old Testament, Abraham, the biblical father of the nation of Israel, was prepared to sacrifice his son, Isaac, to God on this stone. As God's "chosen people," the Jews regarded both the temple and the city of Jerusalem as their most holy site and the center of their faith.

The Temple of Solomon survived for four hundred years. Then, in 586 B.C.E., it was destroyed by the Babylonian king Nebuchadnezzar, who drove the Jews into exile. The Jews returned to Jerusalem and rebuilt the temple in 515 B.C.E., and this "Second Temple" survived until C.E. 70. By this time, though, two new claimants to Jerusalem were on the scene.

The Roman Empire

One set of claimants was the Romans. The Roman Empire lasted for about five centuries. It began in 27 B.C.E., after years of civil war, when the Roman senate confirmed Gaius Octavius as the sole emperor. The empire had its roots much earlier, however. During the period historians call the Roman Republic, which dated from 527 to 509 B.C.E., Rome had taken over other parts of Italy and nearby territories. Rome expanded greatly during the period of the empire. In time, it dominated the entire area around the Mediterranean Sea, including much of Europe.

In 63 B.C.E. Jerusalem and the surrounding nation of Palestine fell under the control of Rome. In the decades that followed, life under Roman rule became increasingly difficult for Jews, who were persecuted and forced to pay high taxes to Rome. At about the beginning of the Common Era, a radical Jewish group known as the Zealots formed. In C.E. 66 the Zealots launched a revolt against Rome, known in Jewish history as the Great Revolt. The revolt ended in the year 70,

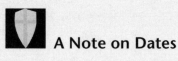 **A Note on Dates**

In referring to dates, historians distinguish between the Common Era, beginning with the year 1, and the time before year 1, or Before the Common Era. Many texts use the initials A.D., which stands for the Latin expression *anno Domini,* or "the year of our Lord," in referring to the Common Era. They use B.C., which means "before Christ," to refer to the era before the birth of Christ. Many modern writers, however, believe that these designations seem to exclude people who are not Christian, so they prefer designations referring to the Common Era. Thus, instead of A.D. they use C.E., and instead of B.C. they use B.C.E. By convention, B.C.E. is placed after the year, while C.E. is placed before the year.

when Roman troops laid siege to Jerusalem, massacred the Jews, and destroyed the Second Temple. In 132 the Romans built on the site their own temple to their god Jupiter.

Christianity

The other new group that took an interest in Jerusalem in the first century was the early Christian church. Early Christianity, which formed around the teachings of Jesus Christ, began as a sect of Judaism and shared many of its beliefs. But as time went on Christians separated themselves from Jewish traditions and practices. The Christian church laid claim to Jerusalem as its holy city, for it was the site of many of the key events in the life of Christ. (For this reason, the region around Jerusalem and Palestine is often called the Holy Land.) In particular, it was the site of the Holy Sepulchre, the tomb of Christ. Rescuing the tomb of Christ from the Muslims would become a key motivator for many of the Crusaders hundreds of years later.

As Christianity spread and its influence over the people in the region grew, it became more and more of a threat to Rome, which practiced a pagan religion, worshiping many gods. For three centuries Christians suffered from persecution at the hands of the Romans. This persecution ended abruptly when the Roman emperor Constantine I, who ruled from 306 to 337, could see that Christianity was gaining in power and influence. In 313 he converted to Christianity, declared it the official religion of the empire, and ruled from the eastern capital of Byzantium, which he renamed Constantinople in his own honor. Some historians believe that his conversion was sincere; others believe that he converted only to retain power over the empire. In 391 and 392 the emperor Theodosius I made Christianity the sole legal religion in the empire. These events gave Christians more control over Jerusalem and enabled Christianity to spread throughout the region.

The collapse of the Roman Empire

By the fifth century the Roman Empire's boundaries stretched from England in the northwest across Europe and into Asia. Such a large empire was expensive to maintain and hard to control and defend. Communication over these long distances was difficult, and the economic demands of ruling such a large empire weakened Rome.

In the fifth century the Roman Empire finally collapsed. The last ruler of a united Roman Empire was Theodosius I, who reigned from 379 to 395. Just before his death in 395, he divided control of the empire between his two sons, and at this point the empire was united in name only. The western realms continued to be ruled by the emperor in Rome, the capital city, but the throne was weakened by a series of child emperors over the next several decades. The eastern part, called the Byzantine Empire, was ruled by an emperor in the capital city of Constantinople. No emperor was ever again able to control both the eastern and western halves.

In the years that followed this division, the empire in the West was almost immediately attacked and overrun by warlike tribes, including the Vikings from the north and various Germanic tribes from the east. These invasions further weakened the western empire. In 476, when the Germanic warlord Odovacar defeated the last western emperor, the Roman senate declined to name a new emperor. In this way, the Roman Empire ceased to exist in the countries of western Europe.

Europe before the Crusades

What followed was a period of turmoil and warfare but also a period when the individual nations of Europe began to unify and grow stronger. Many of these nations, though, were not really nations. Rather, they were loosely connected federations of provinces and regions that shared common languages and cultures but lacked a sense of national identity and purpose. That would begin to change in the centuries preceding the Crusades.

The Frankish kingdom

Among the most important of these nations was the Frankish kingdom (known today as France) in the region Rome had called Gaul. After the Romans withdrew, the

Frankish kingdom was relatively weak. By the eighth century it included a number of loosely related provinces, including Aquitaine, Burgundy, and large parts of modern-day Germany. But Charles Martel, who reigned as king from 714 to 741, and his son Pepin the Short, who reigned from 741 to 768, formed strong alliances with the Frankish nobles and the church in Rome, and the empire began to become stabler.

The kingdom blossomed under Pepin's son, Charles the Great, or Charlemagne, who ruled from 768 to 814. Charlemagne, a skilled military commander and beloved leader, expanded the boundaries of the kingdom. Under Charlemagne the kingdom dominated western Europe and became a center of learning and culture, as he attracted scholars and artists to his court. Beginning in the tenth century further unification took place under the so-called Capetian kings of France, named after the first, Hugh Capet. He and his successors, especially King Louis VI ("Louis the Fat"), subdued many of the less important nobles who tried to defy them, claimed and enforced a hereditary (usually passed down from father to son) right to the throne, and turned the Frankish kingdom into a major nation-state.

The Viking and French invaders

Meanwhile, in the north, the Vikings from the Scandinavian countries of Denmark, Norway, and Sweden joined the Germanic invasions of Europe in the fifth century. Because of the cold climate of extreme northern Europe, there was not enough farmland to support the population, so this southward migration resumed in full force in the ninth and tenth centuries. The Vikings began to raid England in 787, and in 841 they plundered London, starting an era of conquest of the British Isles. Throughout the ninth century the "Northmen" continued to conduct raids down the Atlantic coast in Normandy (a coastal region of France), around the coastline of the Iberian Peninsula (Spain and Portugal), and into the Mediterranean Sea. They also expanded into the Slavic regions of eastern Europe. While the Scandinavians initially were not as strongly Christian as the rest of Europe, many eventually converted to the Christian faith.

Charlemagne (742–814)

While the reign of Charlemagne, or Charles the Great, predated the Crusades by more than two centuries, he was an important background figure. His life contributed to the ideology, or philosophy, of crusading. For centuries he remained a hero whom many Christian Crusaders strove to imitate.

Charlemagne ruled as king for forty-six years. He was important politically because he gave form to the Frankish kingdom. He was a popular hero and a skilled commander, well loved by his soldiers. In *A History of Europe*, historian H. A. L. Fisher writes:

> To his Frankish warriors he was the ideal chief, tall and stout, animated and commanding, with flashing blue eyes and aquiline nose, a mighty hunter before the Lord. That he loved the old Frankish songs, used Frankish speech, and affected the traditional costume of his race—the high-laced boots, the cross-gartered scarlet hose, the linen tunic, and square mantle of white or blue—that he was simple in his needs, and sparing in food and drink were ingratiating features in a rich and wholesome character.

During his reign, Charlemagne fought for Christianity against the Danes, the Lombards, the Saxons, the Slavs, the Muslims in Spain, and others. In doing so, he helped cement the position of the Christian church, making it a stabler and more powerful institution throughout Europe. In recognition of his role as a fighter for Christianity, the patriarch of Jerusalem (that is, the chief Greek Orthodox cleric) sent him the keys to the holy places in the city, telling Charlemagne that he relied on the king for their defense. This, plus his many victories over enemies of the Christian church, planted a seed that would grow into the Crusades—the belief that it was God's will that Christendom extend its realm and that Europe might one day be called on to rescue the holy city. The legends that surrounded Charlemagne contributed to a way of thinking. In the minds of many Christians, the most heroic person imaginable was a Christian knight bearing the cross and willing to fight and die to protect the faith from nonbelievers.

In England, King Alfred the Great, who ruled from 871 to 899, organized an army and turned back the Danes. Then, in 1066, Duke William of Normandy led an invasion of England—the Norman Conquest—that forever changed the face of the island nation. His successors, Kings Henry I and II, accomplished in England what Charlemagne and the Capetians had accomplished in France. They were strong rulers who turned a collection of dukedoms into a nation-state with more of a national identity. The relationship between England and France, though, was complex. These English kings held as part of their domain large portions of western France. For this reason, England and France were in a near-perpetual state of warfare.

The Holy Roman Empire

A final western power that would play a role in the Crusades was the Holy Roman Empire. This empire was formed in 962 when the German king Otto I was crowned. It lasted until 1806, when the final emperor, Francis II, gave up his title. The Holy Roman Empire had been founded by Charlemagne, who believed that the Roman Empire had not truly ended in the fifth century but rather was suspended. He and his followers, as well as the pope, wanted to restore it to power, so in 800 Pope Leo III crowned Charlemagne as the new Roman emperor.

For the next century and a half, the title was more of a personal honor and carried little political authority. That changed with the coronation of Otto, and for the next nine hundred years the Holy Roman Emperor ruled over a kingdom that consisted largely of Germany but also, at various times, of Austria, Bohemia, Moravia, part of northern Italy, Belgium, the Netherlands, and Switzerland. The emperor was always a German king who, technically, was elected by the German princes and had to be confirmed by the pope. In time, the crown became hereditary.

The political justification for the formation of the empire was that just as the pope represented God in spiritual affairs, the emperor represented God in temporal (earthly) affairs. The emperor, therefore, claimed to be the supreme monarch, or ruler, of all of Christendom. While the Holy Roman Emperor held considerable power, he was never recognized as a supreme temporal ruler of all the Christian nations. Christian countries such as England, France, Denmark, Poland, Sweden, Spain, and others never fell within the boundaries of the empire. One Holy Roman Emperor, Frederick I, or Frederick Barbarossa ("Red Beard"), would lead an army of German knights during the Third Crusade. At the center of the Sixth Crusade was his grandson, Frederick II, who negotiated with the Muslims and won Jerusalem back for Christendom—at least briefly (see "The Third Crusade" and "The Sixth Crusade" in Chapter 6).

In contrast to western and northern Europe, the Byzantine Empire not only survived the breakup of the Roman Empire but also, in the centuries that followed, grew in power and influence. Constantinople became a major world capital, the center of great wealth, learning, and cultural development. Trade flourished from the empire's port cities, especially the capital itself, and the surviving architecture and other artifacts (the man-made objects of a civilization) from the region show its past as a stable, prosperous empire.

Religious separation of East and West

In time the political separation of the eastern and western parts of the Roman Empire led to religious separation as well. After the collapse of the Roman Empire, both parts of the empire remained Christian. In the West the withdrawal of the Romans left behind a power void that was filled by the church. Without strong temporal rulers or fully unified nations, the church became, in effect, the ruler of much of Europe. The concept of a Christian state, often referred to by the Latin phrase *Res Publica Christiana,* was widely accepted. While the separate nations of Europe warred with one another in the centuries that followed, the Christian church became the dominant social, cultural, educational, and political institution.

In the East, the church fell under the authority of the Byzantine emperor. In the centuries that followed, tensions between the two branches of Christianity emerged. Part of the division was cultural. As noted earlier, the West relied on Latin, not just in the church but also in law, government, and learning. The Latin language enabled people educated by the church to communicate with one another, even if they came from different countries or spoke different dialects of the same language. In the East, by contrast, church affairs were conducted primarily in Greek and other local languages. Not speaking the same language, the two branches of the church drifted further and further apart.

By this time, too, the Byzantine Empire had surpassed the West in power, learning, and influence. Without the support of Rome, western Europe plunged into a period of backwardness, leading many historians to refer to the

Middle Ages in Europe as the Dark Ages. For this reason, the Byzantines tended to look down their noses at the Romans. As Terry Jones and Alan Ereira quote in *Crusades,* at one time a high-ranking member of the eastern church told a Roman clergyman that Rome was home to "vile slaves, fishermen, confectioners [candy makers], poulterers [dealers in poultry and game birds], bastards [children born out of wedlock], plebeians [lower classes], and underlings [inferior commoners]"—in other words, that they were all common, lower-class laborers and shopkeepers. For their part, Europeans tended to share the view of one bishop (also quoted by Jones and Ereira) who had visited Constantinople and found the inhabitants "soft, effeminate, long-sleeved, bejewelled and begowned liars, eunuchs [castrated men] and idlers [lazy people]"—that is, they were all weak, lazy, unmanly people who lounged about in fancy clothing. In this climate of distrust and mutual scorn, the two branches of the church competed fiercely over converts to the faith, particularly among the Slavic peoples of eastern Europe. Rome also resented Byzantine churches in its own backyard in southern Italy.

The Great Schism

Finally, in 1054, these tensions reached a snapping point. The eastern branch of the church refused to recognize the authority of the pope in Rome. In response, the pope excommunicated, or expelled, one of the highest-ranking clergymen of the eastern church. (This excommunication was eventually lifted, but not until 1965.) The clergyman had actually been provoking the division by declaring to the other patriarchs (leaders of the eastern church) that supporters of the Roman church were heretics, or believers in false doctrine.

The result was the Great Schism (or split), creating two separate Christian churches. In the West was the Roman Catholic, or sometimes Latin, Church. In the Byzantine Empire was the Eastern, or often Greek, Orthodox Church. In time, various nations developed their own brand of Eastern Orthodoxy, so reference is made to, for example, Russian Orthodox or Armenian Orthodox Christians.

It is important to remember that this division did not lead to bitterness or permanent ill feeling. Despite their differences, the eastern and western churches, like quarreling siblings, retained a kinship with each other that would play a role in the Crusades, particularly the First Crusade, when East and West were initially allies in the fight against the Turkish Muslims. In the meantime, however, Jerusalem fell under the control of the Christian Byzantine Empire.

The emergence of Islam

As if the political and religious situation in the Middle East were not complicated enough, a new claimant to the Holy Land emerged in the seventh century: Islam. Islam was founded in the early seventh century by an Arabic preacher named Muhammad (c. 570–632). In 610 Muhammad heard the voice of the angel Gabriel, which revealed to him the words and prophecies of Allah (from the Arabic *al-ilah,* meaning "the One True God"). In the years that followed, Muhammad, who regarded himself as the last in a line of prophets that began with Abraham and included Jesus, spread these revelations to his followers. These revelations became the basis of the Islamic faith, and a follower of Muhammad became known as a Muslim, from the Arabic expression *bianna musliman,* meaning "submitted ourselves to God." In time these revelations and prophecies were written down in the Islamic sacred text, which is called the Qur'an, usually spelled "Koran" in English texts; the present version of the Koran was written in 651 and 652.

The holiest place for Islam was and still is Mecca (in today's Saudi Arabia), where Muhammad was born and experienced his revelations. Also regarded as a holy place is the city of Medina, 270 miles (434.5 kilometers) to the north of Mecca. Medina was originally named Yathrib, but its name

An engraving depicting Muhammad receiving his call to become a prophet of the Islamic religion. *Corbis. Reproduced by permission.*

A Note on Spellings

The name Muhammad is spelled in various ways, including Mohammed and, especially in older texts, Mahomet. Many words and names associated with Islam and the Middle East have alternative spellings in different English texts. These words are usually Arabic or Persian, and these languages do not use the Roman alphabet. The words, then, have to be transliterated, meaning that they are converted into the Roman alphabet. This process often leads to different spellings, especially because there may be different pronunciations of the words.

These different spellings can become a problem, especially with Internet searches. For example, the Turkish clan that drove the Crusaders out of Jerusalem just before the Seventh Crusade was the Khwarismians. Sometimes, though, the name is spelled Khwarizmians or even Khoreszmians. The Muslim caliph, or ruler, who seized Jerusalem in the seventh century was Umar, but many texts spell the name Omar. Even western names written in the Roman alphabet pose a problem. The name of one Crusader castle referred to in the literature of the time is spelled thirteen different ways. Internet researchers need to take alternative spellings into account when entering key words. In books, these names may be found in different places in an alphabetical index.

Older texts written from a western perspective often refer to Islam as Muhammadanism or Mohammedanism. Muslims regard these words as offensive, because they suggest that Muhammad was a deity, or god, rather than a prophet.

was changed to Medina from the Arabic phrase *Madinat al-Nadi,* or "city of the Prophet." It was at Medina that Muhammad developed his beliefs and first began attracting converts. Jerusalem also held an important place in Islam because it was the site of the Foundation Stone, where Muhammad made a miraculous flight to heaven. In 691 the Muslims built a sacred mosque (place of worship), al-Aqsa Mosque, on a site adjacent to the Foundation Stone. The mosque is next to the site of the Temple of Solomon, which remains sacred to Jews.

The spread of Islam

At that time the lands of Arabia were populated by largely nomadic clans and tribes—that is, people who moved

Thousands of pilgrims pray at the Prophet's Mosque in the holy city of Medina. Every year, hundreds of thousands of pilgrims visit the resting place of the prophet Muhammad, which is inside the mosque. *©Suhaib Salem/Reuters/ Corbis. Reproduced by permission.*

about rather than settling in one location—that competed and fought with one another. The Arabs had played a small role in world history, but after Muhammad, these clans and tribes were united under one banner, with a deep sense of purpose and historical mission, though tensions came to divide Muslims. They believed that they were the successors to the Jews as Allah's chosen people and that Allah required them to spread their faith through conquest.

An illustration from *The History of the Nations* showing the first four caliphs, Muhammad's successors. Under these caliphs, Muslims spread their faith with great efficiency. *Private Collection/The Stapelton Collection/Bridgeman Art Library. Reproduced by permission.*

Under the first four caliphs, or Muhammad's successors, the Muslims spread their faith with great efficiency. (One major sect, or subgroup, of Islam did not recognize the caliphs as legitimate successors to Muhammad. See Chapter 5 on the division of Shiite and Sunni Muslims.) By the 640s they had seized most of the Byzantine province of Palestine (where Jerusalem was located) and Syria, conquered Persia, and overrun Egypt. In 638, after a lengthy siege, the second

caliph, Umar, accepted the surrender of the city of Jerusalem, which was now in Muslim rather than Byzantine hands (see "Muslims and Jerusalem" in Chapter 2). By the year 700, from their capital of Damascus in Syria, the Muslims ruled an empire that stretched across northern Africa and into central India.

The Great Mosque of Córdoba in Spain, where Muslims are known as Moors. *©Vanni Archive/ Corbis. Reproduced by permission.*

Not content, the Muslims turned their attention to the West. In the early 700s they captured the southern regions of the Iberian Peninsula, which included the countries of Spain and Portugal. From there they crossed the Pyrenees into the kingdom of the Franks, but they were driven back at the city of Tours by Charles Martel exactly one hundred years after Muhammad's death. In the early 800s Muslims conquered the Mediterranean islands of Sardinia and Corsica and then added the island of Sicily to their empire in 902. Beginning in the 800s they attacked cities in southern Italy and even advanced on Rome, though they were repelled in the 900s and 1000s by armies led by the popes.

Spanish Islam

During these same years Spanish Christians were limited to the northern part of the Iberian Peninsula, while Muslims occupied the southern regions. Muslims, whom the Spanish called Moors, dominated most of the south from its caliphate, the Umayyad caliphate, based in Córdoba, Spain. (A caliphate is a region or domain ruled by a caliph. "Umayyad" is the name of a family dynasty.) Spanish Christians began to push south to recapture their land. This conflict lasted until the early fifteenth century. At the Battle of las Navas de Tolosa in 1212, a Christian army met and defeated an invading Muslim army from North Africa, and by 1225 only the region around Granada, a city in the far south of Spain, remained under Muslim control. Muslims were finally driven out of Granada in 1492. In the meantime, Spanish Christian kings actively recruited Christian settlers for the reconquered territories, often giving them generous grants of land. This process of recapture and settlement in Spain is known to historians as the Reconquista.

What is important about these events in Italy, France, and Spain is that for more than three centuries, European Christians had come to regard Muslims as enemy invaders and had already engaged in armed conflict with them many times. Christians, both in the East and in the West, believed that Muslims were occupying their holy ground, the same ground to which the Jews also laid claim. Cultures that were in large part defined by religion were clashing, and these clashes would eventually give rise to the Crusades.

For More Information

Books

Chambers, Mortimer, Barbara Hanawalt, Theodore Rabb, Isser Woloch, and Raymond Grew. *The Western Experience.* 8th ed. New York: McGraw-Hill, 2003.

Fisher, H. A. L. *A History of Europe.* Vol. 1, *Ancient and Mediaeval.* Boston: Houghton Mifflin, 1935.

Jones, Terry, and Alan Ereira. *Crusades.* New York: Facts on File, 1995.

MacMullen, Ramsay. *Christianizing the Roman Empire (A.D. 100–400).* New Haven, CT: Yale University Press, 1984.

Ostrogorsky, George. *History of the Byzantine State.* Translated by Joan Hussey. Oxford, U.K.: Blackwell, 1968.

Von Grunebaum, Gustave E., ed. *Medieval Islam: A Study in Cultural Orientation.* Chicago: University of Chicago Press, 1971.

Web Sites

Halsall, Paul. "Crusades and European Expansion." *Introduction to the Medieval World.* http://www.fordham.edu/halsall/lect/med15.html (accessed on August 11, 2004).

Sloan, John. "The Crusades in Levant (1097–1291)." *Xenophon Group Military History Database.* http://www.xenophongroup.com/montjoie/crusade2.htm (accessed on August 11, 2004).

The Holy City of Jerusalem

2

Seismologists—scientists who study earthquakes—often refer to an earthquake's "epicenter": the place just below Earth's crust where the quake starts and from which it spreads. The word "epicenter" could be used as a figure of speech to refer to Jerusalem, the city in Palestine on the eastern shore of the Mediterranean Sea that became the focus of the Crusades. While several of the Crusades never made it to Jerusalem, capturing—or, later, recapturing—the city was always the Crusaders' goal, for Jerusalem was the site of many of the major events in the life of Jesus Christ, founder of Christianity.

The "holy city," though, did not suddenly become an epicenter for conflict in the eleventh century. It had long been a source of conflict among three of the world's major religions: Judaism, Christianity, and Islam. As the site of the Temple of Solomon, the holiest place of worship for Jews, Jerusalem had been the center of Judaism, and it remained so even after the city fell into the hands of the Roman Empire, the Temple of Solomon was destroyed, and the Roman emperor Hadrian built another temple on the site in the second century.

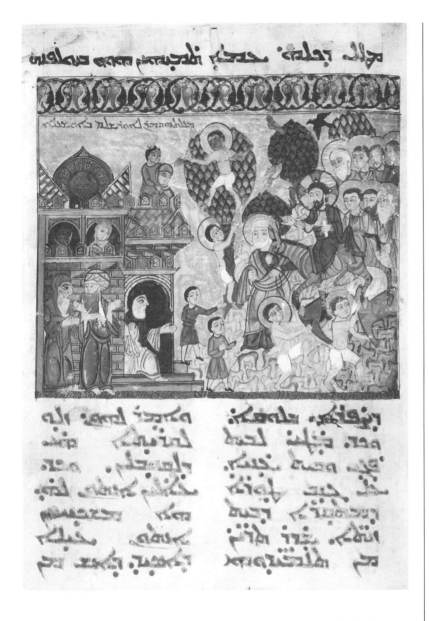

After the Crucifixion (death on the cross) of Christ, the early Christian church laid claim to Jerusalem as its holiest place, for the city was where many of the events in Christ's life took place, including his death, burial, and Resurrection (rising from the dead). Christian control over Jerusalem was confirmed when the Roman emperor Constantine converted to Christianity in 313, declared it the official religion of the empire, and launched a massive construction project in the city. This project included the Church of the Holy Sepulchre, which housed the tomb of Christ, and other churches. The city remained in Christian hands after the Roman Empire collapsed in the fifth century, for it was part of the Byzantine Empire—the eastern part of the old Roman Empire—and came under the religious authority of the Eastern Orthodox Church. Thus, by the time Jerusalem fell to the Muslims in the seventh century, Christians and Jews had long been struggling with the question of who "owned" the city.

For Christians in the East and in the West, Jerusalem was a place of pilgrimage (see Chapter 3 on pilgrimages to the Holy Land). The goal of any devout Christian was to make at least one such journey to the holy places, or shrines, of Jerusalem and do penance (that is, repent for their sins) on the sites where Christ died and was buried. While most Europeans lacked the money to make a pilgrimage, even peasants and commoners would have been familiar with the concept of making such a trip. Because Christ's Crucifixion was central to Christian religious views, Christians were increasingly regarding Jews as people to be scorned. In their view, the Jews were responsible for Christ's death. For their part, Jews regarded Christians as occupiers of their holy city, and they wanted to rebuild their temple there.

Then, late in the seventh century, after Islamic leaders seized control of the city, Muslims built a place of worship, al-Aqsa Mosque, on a site next to the Foundation Stone, the rock upon which Abraham, considered the father of the Hebrew people, had been ready to sacrifice his son to God (see "Judaism" and "The Emergence of Islam" in Chapter 1). Now three major cultural-religious groups were contending for rights to the city. Under these conditions, hatreds were bound to fester and eventually lead to warfare. Since each group regarded the city as among its holiest places, each believed that the presence of the others on holy ground profaned that ground, or made it unholy, so each wanted to drive the others out.

Muslims and Jerusalem

After the death of Muhammad, the founder of the religion of Islam, in the early seventh century, leadership of the faith passed to a series of caliphs, or rulers and leaders of the

Islamic faith. The second of these caliphs was Umar. By the time Umar succeeded to the position, Islam was beginning to expand, and over the next two centuries it established an empire that extended from parts of Spain and Italy in the West, across North Africa and Arabia, and into western Asia. One of the first goals of the caliphs was to gain control of Palestine and Jerusalem. In 636, Muslim forces under Umar clashed with Byzantine forces under the leadership of the emperor Heraclius in a battle on the banks of the Yarmuk River, near the Sea of Galilee. The battle took place in a terrible sandstorm, and the Muslims, accustomed to desert fighting, slaughtered thousands of Byzantine troops. Many of Heraclius's troops were Christian Arabs, but as many as twelve thousand of them deserted and converted to Islam.

When Jerusalem fell to Caliph Umar in 638, most of the city's inhabitants were either Jews or Christians. Initially, they feared for their welfare, but they soon discovered that life under Muslim rule was no worse than it had been under

Not only did Jews and Christians have holy places in Jerusalem, but so did the Muslims. Pictured here is the Dome of the Rock on the Temple of the Mount in Jerusalem, built upon the site where the Muslim prophet Muhammad is said to have ascended into heaven. *©Christine Osborne/Corbis. Reproduced by permission.*

the Byzantine Empire and in many ways was better. Muhammad had taught that both Jews and Christians were "People of the Book." That is, their religions were based on scripture, as was Islam, and Islam was actually a continuation or fulfillment of these other two religions. Islam did not deny the legitimacy of the Old Testament prophets, such as Abraham, nor did it deny the authority of Christ as a prophet. In the eyes of Muslims, Judaism and Christianity were earlier expressions of God's kingdom on Earth. Islam was thought to be the final revelation of God's word, not a denial of Judaism or Christianity.

Accordingly, Jews and Christians were allowed to practice their religions freely and openly. Places of worship, including the synagogues of Jews and the churches of Christians, remained open, and Jews and Christians were even granted some measure of political independence. Muslims welcomed Christian pilgrims (people who journey to sacred places), who continued to come to Jerusalem both from Byzantine lands in the east and Roman Catholic lands to the west. These pilgrims, then and in later centuries, were a valuable source of income for the city.

This policy of tolerance toward Christians was made clear in the treaty between the former leaders of Jerusalem and Caliph Umar. This treaty came to be known as the Pact of Umar. It originated in 638, but over the next three hundred years it expanded while retaining Umar's name. Surviving written versions of the pact vary a great deal, but one that seems most complete dates from sometime in the ninth century. The pact does not refer to the Jews but focuses instead on relations between Muslims and Christians. Historians generally agree, however, that as a pact between a conqueror and a conquered people, it applied equally to Jews and Christians.

In the pact, quoted by Robert Payne in *The History of Islam,* Umar makes clear that Christians would retain the right to practice their religion: "This peace ... guarantees them [Christians] security for their lives, property, churches, and the crucifixes [crosses] belonging to those who display and honour them.... There shall be no compulsion in matters of faith." Umar even refused to unroll his prayer mat in the city's Church of the Holy Sepulchre out of respect for

Miracle of the Holy Fire

Visitors to the Church of the Holy Sepulchre can take part in a ritual that predates the Crusades by centuries. This ritual is called the Miracle of the Holy Fire. It is performed at midday on the eve of Easter each year. Normally, only Eastern Orthodox Christians take part in the ceremony, but Roman Catholics often participate as well, especially in years when Easter falls on the same date for Roman Catholic and Orthodox Christians. (The two branches of Christianity use different church calendars, and Easter is often celebrated on different days.)

During the ritual, church leaders, including the Greek Orthodox patriarch—the chief religious leader—of Jerusalem, go down into the burial area while the congregation holds unlit candles and torches in the darkened church. The faithful believe that the fire of God, symbolizing Christ's Resurrection, is sent down and flames burst forth at the tomb of Christ. Church leaders then emerge from the tomb bearing a lighted torch. From those flames the patriarch lights a candle. The candle is then passed around to Christ's followers in the church. It is believed that Caliph Hakim ordered the destruction of the church in 1009 because he was angered at the Miracle of the Holy Fire.

Christians and the fear that if he did so, Muslims would come to regard the site as their own.

There were some restrictive rules, however. Jews and Christians were required to wear distinctive clothing. They were not allowed to carry weapons or ride on horseback. And while they had to pay special taxes, those taxes were lower than the taxes they had had to pay to the Byzantine rulers. Jews and Christians were also forbidden to hold public office and to study the Koran (the Islamic sacred text) or to imitate Muslims in dress or manner.

All things considered, life for Christians and Jews under Muslim rule, in Jerusalem and other parts of the Middle East, was tolerable at worst and comfortable at best. Meanwhile, trade and business flourished. In fact, for Jews life was actually better. Under the Byzantine Empire, tensions between Christians and Jews in Jerusalem were often high. Christians, who blamed Jews for the death of Christ, were less tolerant of the Jews than the Muslims turned out to be. Byzantine rulers actively sought to convert the Jews to Christianity. For their part, the Jews resented Christians for controlling traditionally Jewish territory, especially in Jerusalem. These tensions had often led to outbreaks of violence and oppression, to the extent that many Jews provided help and information to the invading Muslim army in 638.

From 638 until well into the eleventh century, relative peace reigned in Jerusalem. The exception was during the years 1004 to 1021, when Jerusalem was under the rule of the caliph Hakim (often written al-Hakim). Hakim was insane, and he subjected both Jews and Christians to terrible persecution (prejudice)—although even he allowed pilgrims from the Byzantine Empire and western Europe to visit the holy sites in Jerusalem. After he was removed from office, though, the policy of religious toleration was restored, and peace again prevailed.

Destruction of the Church of the Holy Sepulchre

A crucial event during the rule of Caliph Hakim was the destruction of the Church of the Holy Sepulchre and other Christian buildings in the Holy Land in 1009 and 1010. Included among them were the Church of Saint Anne and the Church of Saint Mary on Mount Zion, the Church of Saint James in the city's Armenian quarter, and the Church of the Ascension on the Mount of Olives. The Church of the Holy Sepulchre, though, was the largest Christian church in the city. Pilgrims to the holy city would have made the church their first destination. Its importance to Christians was that it was on the site where Christ was crucified, buried, and resurrected.

The church had been built in the fourth century by Constantine to enclose the place where Christ was crucified. He had called a meeting in Constantinople with the bishops from that part of the empire. One bishop who attended the meeting was Macarius, the bishop of Aelia Capitolina, the Roman name for Jerusalem. Macarius pointed out that the sites associated with the life and death of Christ were being neglected, largely because of a lack of funds.

Helena, Constantine's mother, was also at the meeting. Like her son, she had converted to Christianity. Accordingly, she made a pilgrimage to the city, bringing with her money

A reliquary containing a particle of the True Cross, on which Jesus Christ was crucified. The True Cross became a central relic of Christendom, a symbol of the Christian faith, and a rallying point for the Crusades. *Armoury Museum, Kremlin, Moscow, Russia/ Bridgeman Art Library.*

and her son's authority. While she was in Jerusalem, she found the place of Christ's Crucifixion, a rock called Golgotha. She also found a nearby tomb that, according to local tradition, had been the site of Christ's resurrection. The emperor then authorized construction of a church on the site—the same site where the Roman emperor Hadrian had built a temple in the second century. When the Roman buildings were being torn down to build the church, a series of tombs was found cut into the rock. One of the tombs was identified as that of Joseph of Arimathea, Christ's uncle, who had helped take Christ's body down from the cross and prepare it for burial. In a cave on the site, Helena found nails from what was believed to be the "True Cross" on which Christ was crucified, and even a plaque saying that the site was Christ's burial place. The True Cross would become a central relic (the remains of a martyr, or one who has died for the faith) of Christendom, a symbol of the Christian faith, and a rallying point for the Crusades.

Although the Church of the Holy Sepulchre was rebuilt in 1048, Pope Urban II would use its destruction earlier in the century to justify the Crusades. Hakim's action would become one in a series of "atrocities," or wicked acts, that the pope declared was happening to Christian sites in the city. He used the destruction of the church to inflame his listeners. Many of the Crusaders who went to the Holy Land did so from a desire to rescue the tomb of Christ from the hands of the infidels, or unbelievers.

Jerusalem under the Franks

Because so many of the early Crusaders were from the Frankish kingdom, or France, Muslims referred to all Crusaders as the Franj, or Franks, and their native land as Frangistan. From the time of the First Crusade until the thirteenth century, Jerusalem was under the control of the Franks for a total of a little more than a hundred years.

This occupation occurred in two distinct phases. The first began when the city fell to the Franks at the end of the First Crusade in July 1099 (see "The First Crusade" in Chapter 6). It remained in Frankish hands until 1187. That year, Muslim forces under Saladin defeated a Frankish army at the Battle of Hattin in July and then laid siege to Jerusalem until it fell in October. The Franks regained control in 1229, after Holy Roman Emperor Frederick II, during the Sixth Crusade, negotiated the Treaty of Jaffa with the Egyptian sultan Malik al-Kamil. When the treaty expired in 1239, the city was briefly occupied by Muslims. It returned to Frankish control in 1241 but was lost once again when a clan of Turkish Muslims, the Khwarismians, attacked the city and drove out the Franks for the final time in 1244.

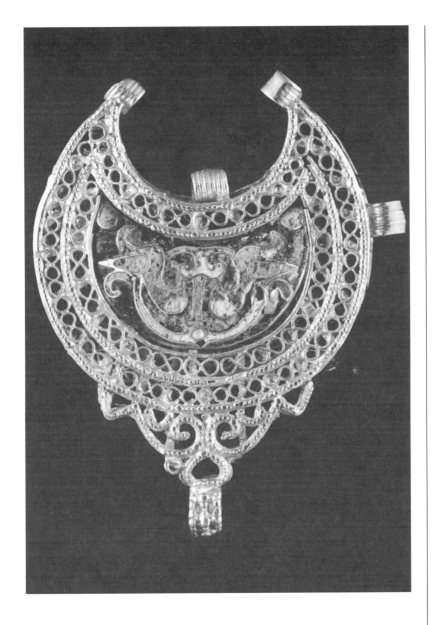

This piece of jewelry dates to eleventh-century Egypt. Such jewelry could have been imported, sent as diplomatic gifts from Byzantine emperors, or made by Byzantine craftsmen who had moved to Fatimid Egypt. *Copyright The British Museum. Reproduced by permission.*

The extent of the changes made to Jerusalem during this relatively short period of time rivaled that of any other period in the city's history. The goals of the Crusaders were twofold. First, they wanted to transform the city into the spiritual and religious "capital" of Christendom by restoring its holy sites. But they also wanted to transform it into a western Christian kingdom in the East. The Crusaders, though, had yet another motive for rebuilding the city. After they breached the city's walls in July 1099, they carried out a mass slaughter for three days. The result was that the city was largely depopulated. Few of the Crusaders remained in the city after the Crusade, and those who did were left with the task of repopulating it.

First, though, they had to rebuild the city. They did not have the funds, and the West seemed unwilling to provide them. Much of the money that financed the rebuilding project came from the abandoned wealth of the Egyptian Fatimids, the ruling dynasty that had controlled the city before the arrival of the Turks. The Crusaders used this wealth immediately to begin restoring or rebuilding the churches that Caliph Hakim had destroyed. Central to this effort was the restoration of the Church of the Holy Sepulchre, which began immediately and took fifty years to complete. On July 15, 1149, the renovated church was consecrated (dedicated to a sacred purpose) once more, and the façade (front of the building) that was consecrated that day can still be seen by visitors to Jerusalem.

Building churches, though, was not the same thing as resettling Jerusalem. To attract people to the city, the Crusaders began to bring back and encourage the pilgrim trade, which had fallen off in the years just before and after the First Crusade. They knew that doing so would attract money, commerce (business), and people, especially permanent settlers, to the city. After the First Crusade, as the journey to the Holy Land became safer for European pilgrims, more and more began to arrive. In time, countless thousands of pilgrims had to be fed and housed each year.

This influx of what amounted to medieval "tourists" created the need for lodgings (called hostels), places for medical care, money exchanges, and markets for goods and services, and the Crusaders constructed these facilities. By the early thirteenth century a French "tour book" titled *La Citez de Jherusalem* shows the extent to which Jerusalem was taking good care of the pilgrim trade. The book not only describes the holy sites but also goes into great detail in directing pilgrims through the streets to markets, money exchanges, hostels, hospitals, and other institutions.

It is difficult for modern historians to know precisely how successful the Crusaders were in bringing people to the city. No reliable statistics exist about the number of pilgrims who traveled to Jerusalem. It is known that the Hospital of Saint John, run by the Knights Hospitallers (see "Knights Hospitallers" in Chapter 9), could accommodate two thousand visitors in a single day, suggesting that the numbers were large.

Another way to gauge the success of the Crusader-builders is to examine the public buildings and monuments they left behind. They strengthened and rebuilt the walls of the city. They constructed a palace, as well as monasteries (religious communities run by monks), convents (housing for nuns), hospitals, bathhouses, covered markets, and other buildings. Presumably, they would not have been able to do so without a major influx of money. Initially, this money flowed to the city largely from the pilgrim trade, though as time went on and more European settlers arrived, other forms of commerce and trade added to the wealth of the city.

A man and woman bathing. As more pilgrims participated in the Crusades, bathing became a more frequent activity among Europeans. *Reproduced by permission of The British Library (Sloane 2435).*

Hygiene and food in the Holy Land

One way in which the cultures of Europe and the Middle East clashed was in attitudes toward personal cleanliness. The Europeans, from colder climates, rarely washed, and, in fact, hated bathing. In contrast, Middle Easterners, from a hot desert climate, bathed frequently. As time went on, though, Europeans took up the habit of bathing, and among the construction projects the Crusaders undertook were more public bathhouses. A bather first went into a heated room. After he worked up a sweat, an attendant would rub him down with soap and towel him off. He would then go to another room, where he could lie in comfort on a couch. The habit of bathing became so ingrained that it was required on some occasions. Anyone who wanted to be admitted to the Knights Templars, for example, had to bathe at a communal bathhouse before the ceremony of admission. Many Arabs in the city were disturbed because Europeans, unlike the Arabs, would often walk about in the bathhouses without towels. The habit of bathing was not limited to men. Women had their own separate bathhouses.

The Franks also saw food in the Middle East that they had never seen before. In addition to meats, game birds, and unusual spices that were unknown in Europe, they ate new types of fruit, including bananas, oranges, lemons, dates, peaches, plums, figs, quinces, and various nuts, such as almonds. They found no vineyards in the Holy Land, for Islam forbade the drinking of wine. The Crusaders planted vineyards and produced wine, which they cooled with snow brought from the tops of mountains in Lebanon and protected by straw as it was transported to the city.

For More Information

Books

Benvenisti, Meron. *The Crusaders in the Holy Land*. New York: Macmillan, 1972.

Boas, Adrian J. *Jerusalem in the Time of the Crusades: Society, Landscape, and Art in the Holy City under Frankish Rule*. New York: Routledge, 2001.

Bridge, Antony. *The Crusades*. New York: Franklin Watts, 1982.

Payne, Robert. *The History of Islam*. New York: Dorset Press, 1987.

Peters, F. E. *Jerusalem: The Holy City in the Eyes of Chroniclers, Visitors, Pilgrims, and Prophets from the Days of Abraham to the Beginnings of Modern Times*. Princeton, NJ: Princeton University Press, 1985.

Periodicals

Hamilton, Bernard. "The Impact of Crusader Jerusalem on Western Christiandom." *Catholic Historical Review* 80 (October 1994): 695–713.

Web Sites

"The Crusader and Ayyubid Period (1099–1250 C.E.)." *The Jerusalem Mosaic*. http://jeru.huji.ac.il/ef1.htm (accessed on August 11, 2004).

Pilgrimages to the Holy Land and Communities in the Holy Land

3

To a Christian, Jerusalem during the Middle Ages (500–1500) was both a place on a map and an idea. On the map, it was a far-off city that Christians, if they could read, knew of from the Bible, and if they could not, they learned about from their priests and bishops. As an idea, though, Jerusalem and other sites in the Holy Land fired the spiritual imagination of Christians, because these sites were the birthplace of their faith. Here could be found the place where Christ had been born, the areas where he had lived and taught, the place where his mother had shed tears for his death, and the sites of his death, burial, and Resurrection. For Christians, Jerusalem and the surrounding region were the holiest places on earth.

The goal of any Christian living at that time was to make a pilgrimage to the Holy Land. At the time of the Crusades, the tradition of making such a trip to a sacred place already had a long history, dating back to the 300s and even earlier. Christians wanted to see the buildings that the Roman emperor Constantine had erected to house the holy sites during his reign in the fourth century. The flow of pil-

The Jewish quarter of Jerusalem. For centuries, Jerusalem and the surrounding region have been sacred places for Christians, Jews, and Muslims. *©James Davis; Eye Ubiquitous/Corbis. Reproduced by permission.*

grims slowed with the Muslim conquest of Jerusalem in the seventh century. Also, continuing political turmoil in Europe up through the ninth century made pilgrimages to the Holy Land the privilege of a select few.

Two events took place that made it easier to make pilgrimages to the Holy Land. First, Hungary, through which pilgrims who traveled on foot had to pass, converted to Christianity. Then the Christian Byzantines extended their empire into Asia Minor and the Balkans. With these friendly nations in control of much of the route, travel to Jerusalem by land became easier, and by about the year 1000 the flow of pilgrims resumed. Early in the eleventh century, Hakim, the Muslim caliph who ruled over Jerusalem, destroyed the Church of the Holy Sepulchre in Jerusalem as well as other buildings that Constantine had constructed. Pilgrims after this time found a different place than the one their ancestors had gone to, but these buildings would be restored after the First Crusade in 1099.

Not every Christian in Europe could afford to make a journey that was as long, exhausting, and expensive as a trip to the Holy Land. Many peasants and commoners had to remain content with visiting sacred sites in Europe—if they could afford to do even that. Those who did make a trip to the Holy Land, therefore, tended to be from the higher classes, including landowners, clerics (members of the clergy), and prosperous merchants, simply because they had the money.

The typical pilgrim was likely to be a member of the nobility—perhaps a count, a baron, a knight, or a landowning vassal (a person who had sworn allegiance to a lord and, in return, obtained the lord's protection; see "The Structure of Medieval Society" in Chapter 9). Women, of course, made the trip, but they rarely went on their own. The pilgrim might have been accompanied by one or more family members; perhaps, too, by companions who had fought with him in battles against the Muslims in Spain. Each pilgrim, if he could afford it, would bring along a servant, and any party of pilgrims would almost certainly have included a priest or monk, who functioned not only as a spiritual adviser but also as a kind of "tour guide."

While a party of pilgrims might have consisted of just a half dozen people, many such small groups often left on pilgrimages together. Also, parties of pilgrims would encounter others along the route and travel together for greater safety. Thus, a caravan of pilgrims often included a great many people, perhaps dozens or more, and the number grew as the pilgrims proceeded. Occasionally, the numbers were much higher. One group, led by Duke Richard II of Normandy, was reported to have consisted of seven hundred pilgrims. In 1064 and 1065 a group of bishops

Women, Pilgrimages, and the Crusades

Because of the difficulties and dangers of the journey, pilgrims tended to be men, but many women made the journey with the same enthusiasm as men did. Much of what historians know about pilgrimages comes from women who wrote about the journeys, such as Etheria of Aquitaine (a region in France), who made the pilgrimage in the fourth century.

Many women accompanied the leaders of the Crusades. During the First Crusade, the wives of Baldwin of Boulogne and Raymond of Toulouse traveled with their husbands. Eleanor of Aquitaine went along with her husband, King Louis VII of France, during the Second Crusade, and Richard I of England married Berengaria, daughter of the king of Navarre, while en route to the Third Crusade. Many of the

women who went suffered great hardships. Some were killed during battles. Others died of disease, including a large number during the siege of Antioch in the First Crusade. Some went along as prostitutes. Others served in such roles as cooks and washerwomen. Interestingly, whenever the Muslims accidentally captured a washerwoman, they always returned her unharmed.

There also are many reports that women took part in battles. They often provided water, wine, and food to the troops or carried stones used as weapons during sieges of castles or cities. One report tells of a woman who was helping fill up a moat during the Third Crusade when she was struck by an arrow. As she lay dying, she insisted that her body be used to help fill the trench.

and nobles led a German pilgrimage whose size was estimated by people at the time at between seven thousand and twelve thousand.

Penance

The chief purpose of a pilgrimage was to do penance, or repent for sins. According to church teaching, sinners could achieve salvation in heaven by showing that they were sorry for their sins, confessing them to a priest, and then offering penance to acknowledge that their sins were offenses against God. Frequently, penance consisted of prayer or giving aid to the poor, but another way to repent was to go on a pilgrimage. The journey itself, because it was so difficult, was part of the penance.

A pilgrim to the Holy Land had to prepare carefully for the journey. Pilgrims first had to confess their sins to a priest, and the priest had to approve the pilgrimage. Without this approval, the pilgrim could not gain any spiritual benefit from the journey. A pilgrim also had to take a public vow before the priest. This vow marked the official beginning of the pilgrimage. The priest would list the specific places the pilgrim was to visit. He would then bless the pilgrim and offer a mass. Later, when the pilgrim returned, the priest would declare that the vow had been fulfilled and that the pilgrim was pardoned of the sins that had required the pilgrimage.

Preparations

A pilgrimage to the Holy Land took months. Typically, European pilgrims would start as soon as they could in the spring and hope that they could make it to the Holy Land, visit the sites, and return before winter, though problems such as ill-

A detail of the *Map of Christian Holy Lands* floor mosaic. This map depicts several sites in the Holy Land that pilgrims were required to visit during their trip to Jerusalem.
© Lindsay Hebberd/Corbis. Reproduced by permission.

ness frequently caused delays. Accordingly, a pilgrim had to make many arrangements before departure. One was to raise enough money to make the journey. A noble or other prosperous pilgrim who wanted to travel in style might spend up to an entire year's income to make the journey. Poorer pilgrims often spent much more than a year's income and often relied on donations and support from their families. Landowners often financed the journey by mortgaging their estates (that is, borrowing money on them) or a portion of them. Others sold personal property to raise the money needed.

After the money was raised, the question arose as to how the pilgrim would keep personal affairs in order during a long absence. Shopkeepers and merchants had to find someone to run their businesses. A noble had to find someone to manage his estate. If the noble was entangled in a dispute with a rival noble, plans had to be made for the defense of the estate. This responsibility would often fall to a relative who was a knight. A noble or vassal also had to see to it that any additional duties he had were taken care of. For example, a vassal who also served as a magistrate, or judge, on his lord's estate had to make arrangements for this task to be fulfilled.

There was always the possibility that a pilgrim would die during the journey. With that in mind, many landholders donated their land to a monastery (a religious community run by monks). Their donation was made with the provision that when they returned, they would continue to receive the income from the land until their death. If they died during the pilgrimage, the monastery would own the land, but any income from it would be used to support the pilgrim's widow and children during their lifetimes. Writing a will was a privilege for only a few during this time. All pilgrims, however, were allowed to write wills. This was not an empty precaution. A cemetery outside Jerusalem held the bodies of many pilgrims who did not survive the journey.

Departure

After the ceremony of taking the vow, a pilgrim would typically depart on foot. A noble would often be followed by dozens, if not hundreds, of well-wishers and family members for the first mile or two. After proceeding for a few miles on foot, pilgrims with means would then gather their horses; pack animals; and, in some cases, wagons and continue the journey on horseback. Poorer pilgrims, of course, would walk all the way to the Holy Land if they took the overland route.

Before the Crusades, most pilgrims did, in fact, travel by land. Their route depended on where they started the journey. Eventually, pilgrims from countries such as France or from the Holy Roman Empire would reach eastern Europe. After traveling through the kingdom of Hungary and the Balkans, they would arrive at Constantinople, the capital of the Byzantine Empire. They then would travel across Anatolia, a region in western Asia Minor, and over the Taurus Mountains to Antioch, a Syrian seaport at the extreme northeastern tip of the Mediterranean Sea. From there they would proceed down the eastern coast of the Mediterranean through western Syria to Palestine and on to Jerusalem. A pilgrim from France faced a journey of some 1,500 or more miles (more than 2,400 kilometers), at the rate of perhaps 25 miles (or about 40 kilometers) a day. If all went well, the journey would take at least two hard months, but rarely did everything go as planned.

At about the time of the Crusades, many pilgrims were making the journey by sea. By this time the Turks were in control of much of Asia Minor, and they harassed Christian pilgrims. Pilgrims also knew that the Turks had fought the early crusading armies that had taken this route. One of the ironies of the early Crusades is that they were fought in part to keep the overland route to the Holy Land open. While the First Crusade succeeded in capturing Jerusalem, the overland route became more dangerous than it ever had been before. At the same time that the Crusaders were fighting to keep the Holy Land open, many pilgrims were actually en route to the Holy Land by sea.

These pilgrims would converge on one of the port cities along the Italian coast, typically Venice. By about the twelfth century Venice was a major maritime power and the chief point of departure for pilgrims, and the city derived much of its income catering to the pilgrim trade. After the Crusades, official guides to the Holy Land were appointed, licensed, and paid by the city. The city was expensive, so pilgrims arriving there would have to find accommodations suited to their means. A noble would have little difficulty affording comfortable lodging. A poorer pilgrim had to make do in a hostel (an inexpensive sleeping place) or even sleep on the ground outside the walls of the city.

The next step was to book passage on a ship. On the city square, tables were set up, one for each ship planning to depart to the Holy Land. Pilgrims would simply approach one of the tables and buy their tickets. Payment had to be in Venetian gold ducats, and money changers were everywhere, ready to exchange into the local currency whatever money the pilgrims had brought—for a fee, of course. Passage on a ship cost about sixty ducats, though poorer pilgrims were often able to book the worst shipboard accommodations for thirty ducats. They would then board a ship, which would sail down the Adriatic Sea to the eastern Mediterranean and onward to one of the port cities on the Levant, the European term for the countries that bordered the eastern Mediterranean. Along the way the ship would make port at islands such as Cyprus to stock up on provisions and provide some rest for weary travelers.

Dangers

A trip to the Holy Land was dangerous, more so the farther a pilgrim traveled away from home. In Europe the roads were still fairly good. People usually welcomed pilgrims to their towns (many of which also contained sacred sites that pilgrims wanted to visit), for the pilgrim trade was a source of income for them as well. Sometimes these towns were the destination of pilgrims who were not headed to the Holy Land. Often pilgrims found hospitality at castles and farms along the way.

The first real danger facing the pilgrims who took the land route to Italy was crossing the Alps. Although pilgrimages started in the spring so as to take advantage of favorable weather, crossing mountainous terrain was always risky. A spring snowstorm could blow up, rivers could rise above their banks during the spring thaw, and bridges were often weakened by the ravages of winter. Whatever route they took, pilgrims confronted the danger of injury or illness, and many arrived in the Holy Land sick or exhausted from the journey. Some ran out of money. A drought during the summer could make food scarce, thereby causing it to become more expensive to purchase. Those who traveled by sea also had a long and difficult journey. Storms at sea could capsize the ships and send pilgrims to their deaths.

One constant danger was bandits. Pilgrims were easy targets, for they typically traveled with few defenses, although a nobleman and his companions might be armed, and prosperous merchants sometimes hired armed guards. Bandits knew that the pilgrims carried money and luxury goods to trade for food and other supplies along the way, and many robbers made a good living off them. Matters were no easier at sea. Pilgrim ships were frequently the prey of pirates, and the commanders of these ships had to go out of their way to avoid areas where pirates were known to lurk.

Another problem related to banditry was extortion. Along the way, local landowners and even entire villages demanded "toll" money for safe passage. Anyone who resisted paying the toll might be killed or at least mugged for money. In the Alps many local nobles held bridges and demanded a toll from pilgrims before allowing them to cross.

Once a pilgrim reached the Holy Land, conditions did not improve. Muslim bandits patrolled the roads leading to Jerusalem and robbed pilgrims when they were almost within sight of their goal. The large group of German pilgrims mentioned earlier in the chapter had to do battle with Arab bandits when they were just two days from Jerusalem. Fighting off the Arabs as best they could, they took shelter in a nearby deserted village and were saved only when Egyptian troops came to their rescue and escorted them to Jerusalem. In fighting the Arabs, though, the pilgrims broke with the tradition that they were to avoid violence because of their pious undertaking. Some historians regard this battle, in which they combined war with a religious mission, as a foreshadowing of the Crusades. After the Crusades, when Jerusalem was restored to Muslim hands, many Christians, even knights, joined Arab bandits in this profitable enterprise.

Arrival

Upon arriving in Ramleh, usually one day's journey from the last stop in Jerusalem, pilgrims were issued instructions. They were always to show Christian charity, patience, and tact. They were to avoid any behavior that could be considered aggressive or offensive. They were not to enter a mosque (a place of worship for Muslims), and they were to stay away from Muslim graveyards. They were always to travel in groups to protect themselves from bandits and pickpockets. Nobles had to be reminded not to engrave their coat of arms into walls and other objects at holy places as well as at inns; graffiti was a problem even a thousand years ago. In particular, pilgrims were not to carry off pieces of holy places or relics, remnants of objects that were held sacred because of their association with saints, though many ignored this instruction and took away with them objects such as stones found at the holy sites.

Typically, visitors arrived at the gates of Jerusalem around nightfall, having left Ramleh in the morning. They paid an admission fee at the Gate of David at the western edge of the city and proceeded to the Hospital of Saint John. The "hospital," which today would be called a hostel, was run by an order of monks who came to be known as the Knights Hospitallers and who would play a role as warrior-monks during the Crusades. At the hospital, pilgrims could get accommodations, and those who were ill or injured could receive medical care.

The sites

The next morning most pilgrims headed directly for the Church of the Holy Sepulchre, the most sacred site in the city. To get there, they may have walked down the Via Dolorosa, or Street of Sadness. This was the route that Christ had taken when he carried his cross to his Crucifixion. All along the way, shopkeepers and street merchants, hawking their products, tried to attract the attention of the pilgrims. Many of the pilgrims were crying in religious ecstasy or singing hymns. A visit to the holy sites in Jerusalem was a noisy and raucous affair, not a quiet and reverential experience.

The Church of the Holy Sepulchre had been built by Constantine and his mother, Helena, in the 300s. Legend holds that she discovered the True Cross, the cross on which Christ was crucified, in the rubble of a demolished Roman

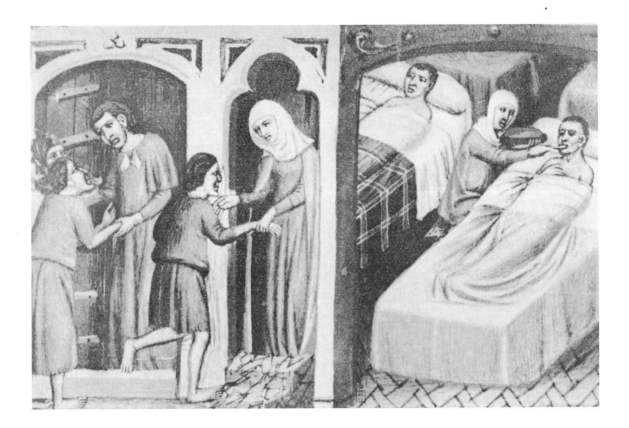

temple. The church was a jumble of shrines and chapels, many of them maintained by Christian sects such as the Nestorians, the Armenians, the Jacobites, and the Coptic Christians. Within the immense building, pilgrims could see many of the places connected with Christ's death. They were often amazed that these places were close enough to one another that they could be enclosed in a single building.

Once inside, they were awed by the places where Christ had been crucified and buried. They could see the hole on Mount Calvary where the cross had been planted in the ground. They viewed the places where Joseph of Arimathea and Nicodemus had taken Christ's body down from the cross and prepared it for burial, where Jesus had appeared to Mary Magdalene, and where his mother had grieved for him. They stood on the spot where the Roman soldiers had divided Christ's garments. To see the tomb of Christ, a pilgrim had to wait for a Muslim to unlock the door. This was a custom that predated the Crusades and continued into modern times. For

A thirteenth-century painting of monks and nuns welcoming travelers and caring for the sick who had arrived in Jerusalem for pilgrimages to the holy sites found within the city. ©Bettmann/Corbis. Reproduced by permission.

Reliquary of the True Cross. Legend holds that Constantine's mother, Helena, discovered the cross, on which Jesus Christ was crucified, in the rubble of a demolished Roman temple. *©Werner Forman/ Corbis. Reproduced by permission.*

a devout Christian pilgrim, arriving at Christ's tomb after months of hardship and danger was to reach the center of the world—indeed, the center of the universe.

Most pilgrims wanted not just to see the church but to spend the night there and hear mass the following morning. Priests and monks hoped that they would be granted the privilege of saying mass in the church. Many young nobles came to the church to be knighted. Pilgrims who were fortunate enough to spend the night discovered that they were locked inside until the following morning.

The Church of the Holy Sepulchre was not the only holy site in Jerusalem. There were many others, but at least two were almost certain to be on a pilgrim's itinerary, and both were located on the Mount of Olives. The first, the Tomb of the Virgin, was regarded as the burial spot of Christ's mother, Mary, and was located at the foot of the mount. The second, the Church of the Ascension, was on the Mount of Olives itself. This chapel was built on the place said to be where Christ had ascended into heaven after his death.

Christian pilgrims to the Holy Land would take in other sites as well, depending on the amount of time they had, the state of their purse, and the list of sites they had been instructed to see when they took their vow. Many went to other cities in Palestine, such as Jaffa, and some went as far as Egypt to see sites mentioned in the Old Testament. Among the most common places, other than Jerusalem, was Nazareth, Christ's childhood home. At Nazareth pilgrims would have seen the site of the Annunciation, where an angel had told Mary that she was to give birth, and the basilica that was built over the site. Although the Muslim caliph Hakim had ordered that this church be destroyed in 1010, the Crusaders rebuilt it in 1101. Also in Nazareth was Mary's house, which had been turned into a basilica in the sixth century. Tradition holds that a third site in Nazareth, Saint Joseph's House, was where Joseph and Mary had wed.

Chapel of the Innocents

A site that pilgrims could visit in Bethlehem was the Chapel of the Innocents. The chapel, which contains numerous bones, memorializes the Slaughter of the Innocents—the killing of children in and around Bethlehem by the Judean king Herod. When Herod learned of the birth of Christ and the prophecies that he was the Messiah, or the savior of the Jews, he was determined to put an end to this threat to his power. He ordered that all male children under the age of two years be killed. Biblical historians debate the number of children who were actually killed. Some put the number at thousands, and others believe that there were as few as twelve.

Christian communities in the Holy Land

In Bethlehem pilgrims visited the Church of the Nativity, built on the spot—a cave—where Christ had been born. At the Church of the Nativity, they would have seen the tomb of Saint Paula of Bethlehem, buried under the church at her death in 404. In 385 Paula (also known as Paulina and Pauline the Widow) traveled with her daughter, Eustochium, on a pilgrimage to Egypt and the Holy Land. The two women settled in Bethlehem, where they built a convent (a home for nuns) and a hospice (a guesthouse) for other pilgrims. Paula was the first abbess of the convent, and after her death her granddaughter, also called Paula, took over the convent, which continued to operate at the time of the Crusades.

While in Bethlehem, pilgrims could also find accommodations at another Christian community. This was the monastery built by Saint Jerome, one of the major fathers of the Christian church. Jerome first traveled to the Holy Land in about 373, and he was ordained a priest at Antioch. After spending time in Constantinople and Rome, he returned to the Holy Land and, like Saint Paula, settled in Bethlehem in 386. There, with the women's help, he built a monastery, where he wrote treatises about Christianity until his death in 420.

The convent of Saint Paula and the monastery of Saint Jerome were typical of the types of accommodation available to pilgrims in the Holy Land. As noted earlier, visitors to Jerusalem could find hospitality at the Hospital of Saint John, and these and other Christian institutions were welcome stops for weary and poor pilgrims. Throughout the region could be found monasteries, convents, and Christian churches run by various sects, or subgroups, of Christianity, as well as by the Eastern Orthodox Church. When the Crusades began, European Christians believed that these and other Christian communities in the Holy Land were under threat and that Muslims were guilty of terrible crimes against their members. It was to protect not only the sacred sites but also these Christian communities that the Crusades were launched.

For More Information

Books

Erdmann, Carl. *The Origin of the Idea of Crusade*. Translated by Marshall W. Baldwin and Walter Goffart. Princeton, NJ: Princeton University Press, 1977.

Fossier, Robert, ed. *The Cambridge Illustrated History of the Middle Ages.* 3 vols. New York: Cambridge University Press, 1986–1997.

Labarge, Margaret Wade. *Medieval Travellers: The Rich and Restless.* New York: Norton, 1983.

Riley-Smith, Jonathan. *The Oxford Illustrated History of the Crusades.* New York: Oxford University Press, 1995.

Sumption, Jonathan. *Pilgrimage: An Image of Mediaeval Religion.* London: Faber and Faber, 1975.

Periodicals

Bull, Marcus. "The Pilgrimage Origins of the First Crusade." *History Today* 47, no. 3 (March 1997): 10–15.

Web Sites

Bréhier, Louis. "Crusades." *The New Catholic Encyclopedia.* http://www.newadvent.org/cathen/04543c.htm (accessed on August 11, 2004).

The Christian Crusades. http://gbgm-umc.org/umw/bible/crusades.stm (accessed on August 11, 2004).

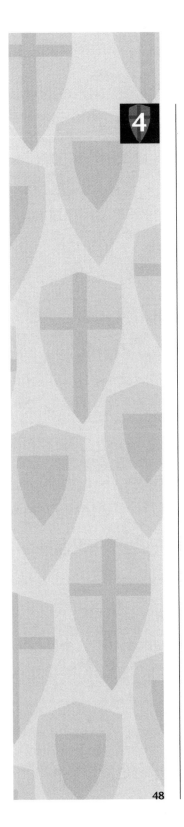

Origins of the Crusades

The Crusades did not happen spontaneously or as a result of a particular event. A number of factors came together to create the political, social, religious, and economic environment that enabled the "crusading spirit" to take root and spread throughout Europe. Although enthusiasm for crusading periodically cooled, it also revived in response to events in the Middle East.

The arrival of the Seljuk Turks

The sands of the Middle East had shifted many times throughout the first thousand years of the Christian era. Jerusalem, the ancient center of Judaism, fell under the control of the pagan (one who worships many gods) Roman Empire and then became a Christian city under the Roman emperor Constantine and his successors. After the breakup of the Roman Empire in the fifth century, the city was controlled by the Eastern Orthodox Church and the Byzantine Empire. Then it fell to the Muslims in the seventh century, and in the centuries that followed it was ruled by the Muslim dynasty of Egypt (see "The Spread of Islam" in Chapter 1).

The sands were destined to shift once again with the arrival of the Seljuk Turks in the eleventh century. The Byzantines gave the name "Turk" to the people who occupied a large area in central Asia. The Turks were primarily a nomadic people (that is, they moved about rather than settling in one place) who belonged to any one of a number of tribes or clans. In the tenth century they converted to the Islamic faith and became part of the Muslim empire.

One of these nomadic clans, the Seljuks, was large and powerful. The Seljuks proved to be ungovernable—that is, they could not be controlled—and they began to overrun the Middle East. In 1055 they seized Baghdad, the capital of modern-day Iraq but at that time in the nation of Persia. They then gained power over Syria and the rest of Persia. They also launched an invasion of the Byzantine nation of Armenia, located east of Turkey and north of modern-day Iran. Finally, in 1071, a little more than two decades before the start of the Crusades, they overthrew the Fatimids, the name of the Egyptian Muslim dynasty that ruled Jerusalem. Once again, control of the Holy Land was in different hands.

The Byzantine emperor, Romanus IV Diogenes, was determined to turn back the Seljuk threat to the shrinking Byzantine Empire. He assembled an army, which met the Seljuks near the city of Manzikert in Armenia in 1071. The Seljuks were tough, experienced warriors, and although they were badly outnumbered, they soundly defeated the Byzantines and captured the emperor.

This event was a turning point. After the historic Battle of Manzikert, the Byzantines were unable to stop the Seljuks, who continued to take lands belonging to the Byzantines in Asia Minor. (Asia Minor is the peninsula of land on the western edge of Asia, bounded on the north by the Black Sea, on the south by the Mediterranean Sea, and on the west by the Aegean Sea.) Of particular importance was the loss of key cities such as Antioch (the ancient capital of Syria but now part of Turkey) and Edessa (now the city of Urfa in Turkey). After centuries of stability and prosperity, the Byzantine Empire shrank to a much narrower area surrounding the city of Constantinople.

A cry for help

People in Europe were alarmed by these developments for two reasons. First, they were worried that the Seljuk Turks would deny Christians access to Jerusalem, a holy city. At a time when Europeans identified so strongly with the church and believed that one way to win salvation in heaven was by making a pilgrimage (a journey to a sacred place) to the Holy Land, this was a troubling development (see Chapter 3 on pilgrimages to the Holy Land). They were partly correct. While the Seljuks did not officially cut off pilgrim traffic from the West, their presence made the journey far more difficult than it had been. Pilgrims passing through the region often needed armed escorts because of bandits. In nearly every small town along the way, the local ruler would demand money for safe passage. Pilgrims to the Holy Land returned to Europe with tales of great danger and enormous expense. Danger and expense had always been part of the penance, or atonement for sin, of a pilgrimage, but the Seljuks made matters worse.

Westerners were also concerned about the fate of the Byzantine Empire. They knew that if Constantinople fell to the Muslim Seljuks, the empire probably would collapse entirely. They wanted the empire to remain stable and strong, for it served as a buffer between the Muslim empire and the Christian countries of Europe. As things stood, Muslim invaders had already attacked Italy, France, and Spain. They had a toehold in Europe with a caliphate (an Islamic ruling power) in Córdoba, Spain. With no Byzantine Empire to hold the Muslims in check, Europe would face an even greater threat. Some historians believe that the Europeans were correct and that if they had not fought the Muslims during the Crusades, these invasions of Europe would have been more frequent and, in the end, more successful. Much more of Europe could have become part of the Muslim empire.

Furthermore, even though the Eastern Orthodox Church and the Roman Catholic Church had split, the Eastern Orthodox Church was still Christian, so western religious and political leaders did not want to see it fall to an unfriendly empire. As early as 1074 Pope Gregory VII, the leader of the Roman Catholic Church, wanted to reunite the branches of the Christian church. He made plans to lead a Christian army to come to the aid of the East by driving the Seljuks out, but he never put the plan into effect. Gregory and his successors saw events in the East as a way perhaps to reunite the church or, at least, to force the Greek Orthodox Church to submit to Rome.

In 1081 the fortunes of the Byzantine Empire began to improve when a new emperor, Alexius I Comnenus, was crowned. Unlike some of his predecessors, Alexius was a competent ruler and a skillful military leader. Under his leadership, the Byzantines were able to stop the advance of the Seljuks. He knew, though, that he would never be able to drive them out entirely and reclaim Byzantine lands without help from the West. He had to enlarge his army, and he concluded that the only way he could do so was with mercenary soldiers, or hired troops, from the West. Alexius decided that his most promising course of action was to employ French knights to expand his own army, though he would take any help he could get.

Byzantine Emperor Alexius I Comnenus wrote letters to lords and nobles in the West asking for assistance in ousting the Muslims and the Turks from the Holy Land. *Photograph courtesy of The Library of Congress.*

Accordingly, Alexius wrote letters to lords and nobles in the West, asking for assistance. As a good politician, he knew that his appeal would be ignored if he based it entirely on a desire to regain his own empire. Instead, he appealed to western Europe's Christian feelings. He described Muslim violence against Eastern Christians. He painted a picture of Christians in the East needing to be delivered from the tyranny, or domination, of Muslim overlords. He argued that it was not acceptable that the holy places of the East should be in the hands of Muslims and Turks, who were not Christians and therefore were considered "infidels," or unbelievers. He raised the image of Muslims denying Christian pilgrims, whether from East or West, access to those holy places.

It is important to note, though, that much of what Alexius claimed was exaggerated, and often false. Moreover,

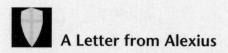

A Letter from Alexius

Here is an example of the letters Alexius wrote to the nobles of Europe, describing the evils that he claimed the Turks were committing. This is an excerpt from his letter to Count Robert of Flanders, quoted by Robert Payne in *The Dream and the Tomb: A History of the Crusades*:

> O illustrious count and great consoler of the faith, I am writing in order to inform Your Prudence that the very saintly empire of Greek Christians is daily being persecuted by ... the Turks.... The blood of Christians flows in unheard-of scenes of carnage [killing], amidst the most shameful insults.... I shall merely describe a very few of them....
>
> The enemy has the habit of circumcising [to cut off the foreskin of the penis] young Christians and Christian babies above the baptismal font [a vessel for holy water used at baptism]. In derision [disrespect] of Christ they let the blood flow into the font. Then they are forced to urinate in the font.... Those who refuse to do so are tortured and put to death. They carry off noble matrons [married women] and their daughters and abuse them like animals.

the Muslims who he claimed were guilty of these "atrocities" (or evils) were the Seljuks, not the Egyptian Fatimids who had been in control of Jerusalem for centuries before the Seljuks arrived.

In February 1095 Pope Urban II (c. 1042–1099) was leading a church council in Piacenza, Italy. While he was in Piacenza, a group of diplomatic representatives (political ambassadors) from Constantinople arrived with a direct appeal for help from Alexius. Urban and the other church officials attending the council were deeply moved by the emperor's plea. Immediately after the council, Pope Urban began to make plans to come to the aid of the emperor. The result would be the First Crusade, which ended with the capture of Jerusalem by Christian forces in 1099 (see "The Sermon at Clermont" in Chapter 6.)

Other origins of the Crusades

These were the immediate events that led up to the Crusades. They explain the political situation in Europe and the East, but they fail to account fully for Europe's enthusiastic response to the pope. Throughout Europe, thousands of men

willingly and eagerly "took up the cross" and joined the Crusades. The central question that historians ask about the Crusades is "why?" What were the motives of the Crusaders? Why did Europeans respond as keenly as they did? Can the Crusades be explained by social, economic, or religious factors?

Historians give varying answers to these questions, but all agree that the Crusaders had many motives, or driving

A painting of Pope Urban II proposing the First Crusade in 1095. *©Archivo Iconografico, S.A./Corbis. Reproduced by permission.*

forces. Many people genuinely believed that Jerusalem had to be liberated from the infidel and that access to the Holy Land for Christian pilgrims doing penance for their sins had to be maintained (see "Penance" in Chapter 3). Others could not pass up the pope's offer of an indulgence for going on a Crusade. According to church teaching, at death a person's soul first went to purgatory instead of heaven. Purgatory was a place of punishment for sins committed during a person's lifetime. The time spent in purgatory was a delay in joining God in heaven. An indulgence was a reduction in the length of time spent in purgatory. Indulgences could be earned by, for example, saying certain prayers or performing certain acts. The pope offered a "plenary" indulgence to Crusaders, meaning that they could bypass purgatory entirely and go straight to heaven.

Religious hysteria

In his essay "The Children's Crusade," the historian Norman P. Zacour argues that the Crusades were part of the religious hysteria that from time to time swept through Europe. Zacour reminds his readers that many Europeans in the Middle Ages (500–1500) lived lives that were utterly dreary. Life was insecure, violence was everywhere, and poverty was widespread. In such an environment, people often fell victim to religious hysteria, believing that if this world provided few comforts, the next one would do so. It is no surprise, then, that they responded to Crusade preaching with great enthusiasm. What emerged, according to Zacour, was a kind of mass religious hysteria, or frenzy. Without this hysteria, the Crusades might never have taken place. Two chief instances of this hysteria were the People's Crusade and the Children's Crusade.

The People's Crusade

The People's Crusade, sometimes called the Pauper's Crusade, was really the "First" Crusade, although it is not normally numbered as such. It was led by a wandering evangelist named Peter the Hermit. If the Crusades promised high adventure for noble knights fired with zeal, or enthusiasm, to carry out brave deeds, the People's Crusade was something different. As the historian Franklin Hamilton notes in his book *The Crusades,* "the grand drama of the Crusades opened with a touch of farce." The leading characters in this farce were Peter's ragtag army of commoners and peasants who were swept up in the hysteria of the First Crusade.

Peter's Crusaders were the first wave of Europeans to arrive in the East after Pope Urban's sermons preaching the Crusade. Peter was a small man who wore filthy clothes and went about barefoot. With a long, dark face, he was almost comical, and yet he had power over others. Wherever he went, he attracted hundreds of followers, and his army grew like a snowball as it rolled through France and Germany. But the people he drew to the cause were not knights; instead, they were a varied crowd of peasants, petty criminals, women, children, aged people, knights who had been disowned by their families, and ill people. Peter promised them something their feudal masters, those to whom they had previously pledged their service in return for protection, could not—salvation. They could leave their grim life and find the grace of God, perhaps even personal glory, fighting the infidel in the Holy Land. By the time Peter reached Cologne, Germany, as many as fifteen thousand people were already in his army.

The pope had announced that the First Crusade was to depart for the Middle East in August 1096, but Peter and his followers were impatient to go, so they set out from Germany in April. By this time the People's Crusade had grown even larger. The exact size is a matter of some debate, but estimates range from twenty thousand all the way up to three hundred thousand.

This first wave of Crusaders, often hungry and always badly disciplined, caused nothing but trouble as they traveled to the Holy Land through eastern Europe. They started a riot in Hungary and sacked, or destroyed, the city of Nish, in modern-day Bulgaria. Word of these outrages reached the Byzantine emperor. He sent an armed force to restrain them under the guise of "escorting" them to Constantinople. But fighting broke out between the Crusaders and their escort, and the Byzantines attacked. The People's Crusaders finally submitted, but not before as many as ten thousand had been either killed or taken into slavery. Still, the People's Crusade pressed on.

The disappointment of Alexius when these uncouth warriors began to arrive at the gates of Constantinople in July 1096 can only be imagined. They continued to cause trouble, robbing country estates and looting buildings. Alexius, frustrated and angry, settled them in August in a military camp across the Bosphorus Strait in Asia Minor and pleaded with them to wait to continue with the Crusade until trained men-at-arms arrived from Europe.

However, the People's Crusaders, fired with enthusiasm for their holy cause and always hungry, were not willing to wait. On October 21, 1096, Peter was away in Constantinople. In his absence, a large force of People's Crusaders set out to engage the Turks in battle. Leaving the women and children in camp, they marched straight into a Seljuk ambush. Virtually no one survived the assault. The Seljuks then stormed the camp, and five hours later the destruction of the People's Crusade was complete. A few thousand survivors were ferried across the Bosphorus to safety in Constantinople, but the People's Crusade had come to an abrupt and shameful end. When later Crusaders passed though the area, they reported encountering large hills of bones, all that remained of the People's Crusade.

The Children's Crusade

This type of mass religious hysteria did not end with the People's Crusade. Before the Fifth Crusade early in the thirteenth century, a curious instance of mass religious hysteria arose when the so-called Children's Crusade departed for the Holy Land.

In the early thirteenth century a new and larger class of poor was emerging. The population of Europe was increasing faster than the ability to feed it. Wage labor on farms was becoming more common, leading to unemployment in the winter. The burden of taxes on the poor and near-poor was becoming greater. More and more people were wandering the countryside in search of work and charity. These people often resented the church. They believed that God's people were the poor and dispossessed (homeless), not the wealthy and authoritarian church officials. In this climate, the legends of the Children's Crusade took root and flourished in the popular imagination.

Children getting ready to embark on the Children's Crusade to the Holy Land. After departing on their journey, the children were never heard from again, and their fate is uncertain. ©*Bettmann/Corbis. Reproduced by permission.*

By this time Jerusalem had been lost to the Muslims in 1187, just before the Third Crusade. The Third Crusade failed to win it back. The Fourth Crusade in 1198 went horribly off course and, rather than marching on Jerusalem, attacked the city of Constantinople (see "The Third Crusade" and "The Fourth Crusade" in Chapter 6). Given these failures, many Europeans thought that if armed knights fighting for the pope could not reclaim the Holy Land, perhaps the poor and the innocent could.

It is unclear how much of what is known about the Children's Crusade is true. But the legend is that in May 1212 King Philip of France was holding court when he was approached by a twelve-year-old shepherd boy named Stephen. Stephen was the bearer of an incredible tale. He held in his hand a letter that he said was given to him by Christ with instructions to deliver it to the king. The letter said that the king was to assemble a Crusade and march on the holy city of Jerusalem.

The king dismissed Stephen, but the boy was eager to free the Holy Land, so he traveled through France, preaching his Crusade. Everywhere he went he gathered followers, much as Peter the Hermit had done more than a century earlier. People saw him as a saint. By the time he reached Vendôme, France, up to thirty thousand Crusaders from all ranks of life had left their families and joined him. Not one of these Crusaders was over the age of twelve.

In June 1212 Stephen's army continued on to the port city of Marseilles, France. When they arrived at Marseilles, two merchants, named Hugh the Iron and William the Pig, agreed to transport the children to the Holy Land. A few days out at sea, a storm sank two of the ships, and all aboard were lost. The other five ships survived, but none of the children was ever heard from again.

Eighteen years later a priest who had accompanied the children returned from captivity in Egypt. Only then did Europe learn the fate of its children. After the storm, according to the priest, the surviving five ships, rather than sailing east to the Holy Land, had turned south to the North African country of Algeria. In Algeria the treacherous merchants sold the children into slavery.

Meanwhile, a second Children's Crusade, not knowing the fate of the first, was forming in 1212 in Germany, led by a boy named Nicholas. This group, which numbered around twenty thousand, crossed the Alps into Italy and the port city of Pisa. Many died of hunger and exposure along the way. At Pisa two ships left, carrying some of these young Crusaders to the Holy Land, but nothing was ever learned about their fate. A second group, led by Nicholas, made its way to Rome, where the pope greeted them, told them that they should take up the cross when they were older, and sent them home. Only a few ever made it back, and, again, nothing is known of the rest, including Nicholas. In Nicholas's town, parents who had lost their children turned on the boy's father and hanged him.

The rise of papal power

Another explanation for the Crusades focuses on the increase in the power of the pope, the leader of the Roman Catholic Church. Put simply, the Crusades were a way for popes to assert their authority not only over the church but over temporal (earthly) rulers, such as kings and emperors. In the late ninth and early tenth centuries, the papacy (the office of and institutions surrounding the pope) had been relatively weak, primarily because from 896 to 904, eight different popes reigned. None had a term that was long enough to allow him to expand his authority. Pope Gregory VII, who reigned from 1073 to 1086, was too preoccupied with reasserting the authority of the church in the West to respond to appeals from Constantinople for aid, but he kept alive the hope of reuniting the two branches of Christianity. It would be Pope Urban II who would act on those appeals and use the Crusades as a way to increase church power.

Pope Urban II was a French nobleman by birth, so the Crusades always had a French character and tended to be led by French noblemen. An exception would appear to be Richard I (1157–1199), the king of England, but even Richard, known by his French name Coeur de Lion, or the Lionheart, was more French than English. In the Middle East, Muslims referred to all Crusaders, whatever their national origin, as the Franj, or Franks. Thus, when the pope preached his first Crusade sermon at Clermont, he was speaking in French, primarily to French aristocrats.

At the time, Europe was still largely divided. Although the French king Charles Martel (c. 688–741) had resisted Muslim advances into the Frankish kingdom, and his grandson, Charlemagne (742–814), or Charles the Great, had taken major steps toward strengthening the Frankish empire, the history of Europe during this time was still chiefly the history of barons and nobles at war with one another. Urban, a practical, worldly man, wanted to put an end to this quarreling,

Richard I, the king of England, was just one of the noblemen to lead the Crusades. *©Bettmann/Corbis. Reproduced by permission.*

unite the nations of Europe, ensure that the Muslims in Spain made no further advances, and strengthen the power of the papacy.

The Crusades were a way to accomplish these goals. The Crusades gave Europe a common purpose and sense of direction. They were a way to impose a kind of truce over Europe and redirect its energies into a holy war in the East. They would help reduce Europe's surplus population, not only through combat deaths but also through resettlement in the East, and they would give Europe's knightly class something to do.

The Crusades would also provide an outlet for the second (and later) sons of nobles and landowners. These sons often had few economic prospects of their own because of what was called "primogeniture." Under the system of primogeniture, the estates of nobles and landowners were kept intact, rather than being divided up, by passing wholly to the firstborn son when the landowner died. Many younger sons, especially those who did not want to take up the church as a profession, trained as knights, went on to become Crusaders to the Middle East, and gained estates of their own—for the pope promised that they could keep any territory they won during the Crusade. For the young sons of many French noblemen, this was a powerful and irresistible motive for becoming a Crusader. In areas of Europe where primogeniture was not yet widely practiced, the Crusades served to draw many sons and others who made claims on an estate, often leaving such estates in the hands of a single noble or landowner. Those nobles and landowners would encourage crusading as a way to keep control over their land.

The First Crusade provides a typical example of this desire for territory. As the Crusaders were on the march toward Jerusalem, quarrels began to erupt over the question

Le gran richeces qe dedens troueron.
Le riches pailes, li uar li siglaton.
Li or largant, li peues li carbon.
Bauduin tenoit au poing son copaignon.
Amis dist il, tot ast resor uos don.

Conquis laueis efait ma uncerson.

of who would remain in charge of towns captured along the way. After initial successes at the cities of Nicaea and Dorylaeum (both in modern-day Turkey), two of the Frankish nobles leading the Crusade, Baldwin and Tancred, grew weary of fighting for the cause of the Byzantine emperor, to whom they had made a pledge to restore captured cities. They wanted to capture territory for themselves. To that end, they split their troops off from the main force and headed toward the Mediterranean coast and the city of Tarsus.

The people of Tarsus were largely Armenian Christians, so they welcomed the Crusaders and gladly raised their flag over the city. Baldwin, whose force was much larger than Tancred's, insisted that the city be turned over to him. Seeing that he had little choice, Tancred gave in and headed west along the coast, where he seized the towns of Adama and Mamistra. Like Tarsus, these were Armenian towns whose Christian residents welcomed the Crusaders.

Illuminated manuscript of a knight traveling to the Holy Land during the Crusades. One of the goals of the Crusades was to give Europe's knightly class something to do. ©*Archivo Iconografico, S.A./Corbis. Reproduced by permission.*

Modern-day Urfa, the site of Edessa, one of the Crusader states. Baldwin and his forces were eagerly welcomed as deliverers by the Christian Armenian residents of the city. ©Chris Hillier/Corbis. Reproduced by permission.

Baldwin then set his sights on the wealthy city of Edessa farther inland, where he and his forces were eagerly welcomed as deliverers by the Christian Armenian residents of the city. Baldwin's first step after entering the city was to force its ruler to adopt him as a son. The ruler faced a great deal of resentment from his subjects because of his ties to Alexius, and just a month later an angry mob of them killed him. The mob was most likely provoked by Baldwin, who, as the ruler's heir, was now rich. He married an Armenian princess and settled in as the sole ruler of the city and the surrounding area. In one of their first major victories, the Crusaders, ironically, seized a city from Christian rather than Muslim hands.

The "poetry" of the Crusades emphasizes the efforts of noble knights to gain honor and glory. The "religion" of the Crusades emphasizes efforts of sincere Christians to rescue the tomb of Christ from infidels. But the fact remains that the Crusades were often as much business and politics as they were poetry and religion. Throughout the nearly two-hundred-year history of the Crusades, fighting took up far less time than political infighting, disputes over the crown of Jerusalem and the other Crusader states, and the amassing of wealth. While the popes were not always content with the outcome of Crusades, particularly the failure to recapture Jerusalem, the Crusades helped relocate and redirect much of this misspent energy to the Middle East and a common foe. At the same time, they increased the wealth of many European noblemen.

The Crusade against the Cathars

Another pope who used the Crusades to assert papal authority was Innocent III, who was pope at the time of the Fourth Crusade, which he called in 1198. Innocent, a ruthless, unfeeling pope who craved power, wanted to impose a Christian monarchy over the whole of the known world. He had long wanted the Eastern Orthodox Church to bow to the authority of Rome, and he became obsessed with the reconquest of Jerusalem, which had been lost in 1187.

Not everyone, however, shared the pope's view of papal authority. At the time, a community of Christians who lived largely in southern France refused to acknowledge the pope's authority, either as a temporal or spiritual leader. These people were called the Cathars, a name that means "Pure Ones." In the view of the Cathars, the physical world was evil. They believed that only the poor—in contrast to the worldly and wealthy church—were Christ's true followers. They refused to believe that the sacraments (religious rites) or the words of priests and bishops offered a path to salvation. Many of them wandered the countryside living lives of godliness and poverty. To "correct" the Cathars, the religious order of the Dominican friars, who would themselves lead lives of poverty and simplicity, was formed. But the Cathars refused to yield even to the devout Dominicans.

The pope, though, would tolerate no challenge to his authority. He believed that the Cathars were heretics, or believers in false religious doctrine, and he was determined to wipe them out. His own chilling words, as quoted by Jonathan and Louise Riley-Smith in *The Crusades: Idea and Reality, 1095–1274,* were these:

Let us apply ourselves without cease, and with the help of many, to enforce correction on this vile [wicked] breed of people Ö ulcers which do not respond to treatment with dressings must be cut out with the knife. Those who hold cheap the correction of the Church must be crushed by the arm of secular power.

Accordingly, the pope called a "crusade," urging Christians throughout Europe to rid Christendom of the Cathars. He began by advising the southern French counts of Toulouse and Béiers to rid their provinces of the "enemy" that lived among them. The counts, who were not Cathars, refused to do so. The pope then ordered the northern French to do it instead, promising them that if they went to war against the south, they could keep any property they seized—the same promise Urban II had made to the Crusaders in 1095. By playing the north against the south, the pope was expertly taking advantage of the tension that existed between them. The south tended to be a region of artists, troubadours (singers), and poets. Southerners were apt to see their northern countrymen as ignorant barbarians. The north was more commercial and down-to-earth. Its stereotype of the south was that the people were wild-eyed dreamers.

Enticed by the promise of booty (goods and valuables of the enemy), an army of northern French crusaders led by the Abbot of Cîteaux began launching attacks against small towns in the south of France. Their goal was not to seize territory, as the goal of the first four Crusades had been. Their goal was mass murder. On July 22, 1208, this army attacked the town of Béziers. Elizabeth Hallam, in *Chronicles of the Crusades: Eye-witness Accounts of the Wars between Christianity and Islam,* quotes the abbot, writing later to the pope: "Our forces spared neither rank nor sex nor age. Thus did divine vengeance vent its wondrous rage." Not a single inhabitant of the town was spared. This genocide (deliberate murder of an entire cultural group) against the Cathars and others whom the pope saw as heretics lasted for twenty years. The goal was to stamp out unbelief and assert the church's authority, and the popes used crusading as a way to keep this spirit alive.

The economics of the Crusades

Even during the Middle Ages war was business. It took immense amounts of money to gather and equip an army, transport it long distances, and provision it along the way. Increasing the expense was generally the massive shadow army of pages (youths in service to a knight), squires (attendants to a nobleman), servants, cooks, blacksmiths, priests, bishops, and prostitutes that accompanied the Crusaders.

But unlike today, when troops are paid out of a national treasury funded by taxes, the Crusaders were largely self-financed—that is, the Crusaders paid their own way. For this reason, the various popes who called Crusades depended heavily on the nobles of Europe. It was the nobles, not the kings, who commanded the resources needed to finance a Crusade. An exception to this system came during the Third Crusade, when Kings Richard I of England and Philip II of France enacted the Saladin tithe, referring to the Muslim general whose military successes prompted the Crusade. (A tithe is a tenth and refers to the custom of Christians to donate a tenth of their income to the church.) The tithe was a direct tax levied, or charged, on all church and nonchurch income. This was the first time in western Europe that such a tax had ever been imposed. It introduced permanently a system for collecting and distributing money raised through taxes to pay the expenses of government.

The knights who fought in the Crusades were not paid. They were compensated with the spoils of war (goods obtained or stolen through war) and with land they seized in the Middle East. In the years following the First Crusade, they transplanted the feudal system of Europe to their colonies. Like landowners back in their home countries, these Crusaders ran their affairs from the cities while employing the local people as tenants on farms, groves, and vineyards in the surrounding areas.

All of this, though, took money and supplies from Europe. One of the permanent benefits of the Crusades was that they led to a more organized system of trade, finance, and credit around the Mediterranean Sea. Like many such developments throughout history, what began in the service of war produced immense benefits later during peacetime. At the center of this system were the Italians, especially the merchants of such trading cities as Venice, Pisa, and Genoa. These cities' locations on the Italian coastline made them naturals for the role. They were centrally located and had ready access to ports and shipping lanes along the Levant (the countries along the eastern shore of the Mediterranean) and throughout the region.

At first, the merchants of these cities did not see much profit potential in the Crusades; the first Crusaders carried everything they needed with them and took a route overland to the Holy Land. The Genoese altered that view when they took a gamble and shipped supplies and equipment to the siege at Antioch (see "The First Crusade" in Chapter 6). When the blockade was lifted, they had a permanent foothold there as merchants. The Venetians and the Pisans followed the Genoese and carved out their own market share on the Levant. The Italians invested heavily in fleets of ships to transport goods and people.

At times the Crusades wound up serving purely commercial interests. Good examples are provided by the Third and Fourth Crusades. The Pisans played a major role in the Third Crusade, particularly during the siege of Acre (in modern-day Israel). Leading the siege initially was Guy of Lusignan, king of Jerusalem. Guy at first tried to lay siege to the city of Tyre (in modern-day Lebanon), which was by this time in the hands of the Muslim general Saladin. He gathered a force and marched on the city. Incredibly, though, an Italian named Conrad of Montferrat, a Crusader with a talent for finance, had taken control of the city's business interests and refused to let Guy in. He was happy with the way things were, for he had a monopoly (exclusive ownership) on trade between the city and Europe. Guy then decided to move his forces to Acre to lay siege to that city, and the Pisans offered to help. In exchange for business rights throughout much of the kingdom of Acre, they ferried Guy and his troops to Acre and helped with the siege.

Saladin was in the process of trying, unsuccessfully, to drive Guy and his troops away from Acre when Richard I of England and Philip II of France arrived. With their help, Acre was restored to Christian hands and continued to operate as a key seaport on the Levant during later Crusades. It was this city, a business center, and not the holy city of Jerusalem, that stood as the Crusaders' last outpost in the Middle East when it fell in 1291, bringing an end to the Crusades.

The Fourth Crusade, under the influence of the doge (duke) of Venice, never got anywhere near Jerusalem. Instead, the Crusaders attacked and sacked Constantinople, greatly increasing the power and wealth of the Venetian merchants. The crafty doge was able, in effect, to hijack the Crusade by offering the Crusaders the protection of a fleet of warships in exchange for half of the booty that could be collected. His motive in persuading the Crusaders to attack Constantinople had nothing to do with rescuing the tomb of Christ or freeing the Holy Land. He was angry because the Byzantine emperor was offering more favorable trading terms to the Genoans and Pisans and violating trade agreements with Venice. The sack of Constantinople increased the wealth not only of Venice but also of much of Europe, for the Crusaders returned to their homes with anything of value they could carry from the city.

In sum, the Crusades were not the result of a sudden need in Europe to come to the aid of the Byzantine emperor or solely to reclaim the Holy Land from the Muslims. While these were key factors motivating the Crusades, a number of other factors—religious hysteria, the expansion of feudalism, the custom of primogeniture, growing poverty, social changes, expanding business interests, and the ambitions of popes—all came together at a moment in history. The result was a period of heroic combat and senseless slaughter, of religious fervor and moneygrubbing, of nobility and betrayal, of epic poetry and melancholy tragedy.

For More Information

Books

Hallam, Elizabeth, ed. *Chronicles of the Crusades: Eye-witness Accounts of the Wars between Christianity and Islam.* London: Weidenfeld and Nicolson, 1989.

Hamilton, Franklin. *The Crusades.* New York: Dial Press, 1965.

Mayer, Hans Eberhard. *The Crusades.* Translated by John Gillingham. New York: Oxford University Press, 1988.

Painter, Sidney. "Western Europe on the Eve of the Crusades." In *A History of the Crusades,* vol. 1. Edited by Marshall W. Baldwin. Madison: University of Wisconsin Press, 1969.

Payne, Robert. *The Dream and the Tomb: A History of the Crusades.* New York: Cooper Square Press, 2000.

Riley-Smith, Jonathan, and Louise Riley-Smith. *The Crusades: Idea and Reality, 1095–1274.* London: Edward Arnold, 1981.

Zacour, Norman P. "The Children's Crusade." In *A History of the Crusades,* vol. 2. Edited by Robert Lee Wolff and Harry W. Hazard. Madison: University of Wisconsin Press, 1969.

Web Sites

"Crusades." *Microsoft Encarta Online Encyclopedia 2004.* http://encarta. msn.com (accessed on August 11, 2004).

Medieval Crusades. http://www.medievalcrusades.com/ (accessed on August 11, 2004).

Division of Shiite and Sunni Muslims

5

From a European perspective, the First Crusade ended successfully with the capture of Jerusalem in 1099 by forces from western Europe (see "The First Crusade" in Chapter 6). In the decades that followed, the Crusaders, as these fighters were known, remained in control initially of three major Crusader "states" in the region. These states included not only the Kingdom of Jerusalem but also the County of Edessa and the Principality of Antioch.

After the First Crusade most of the Crusaders returned home. Only a few thousand Europeans remained at any time to administer and defend the Crusader states. What may seem puzzling is how so few Europeans could maintain control of the area. In many respects, the Crusader states were like islands surrounded by nations and empires hostile to them. Most of the people in these nations were Muslims, or members of the Islamic faith founded by Muhammad in the seventh century (see "Islam" in Chapter 1). To the north a large portion of Asia Minor was under the control of Muslim Turks, cutting off the land route from Europe. To the east the Muslims controlled Damascus (in Syria), and to the east

Two Muslim warriors doing battle on horseback. The Crusaders were able to keep control of the Crusader states until the 1130s because the Muslims were sharply divided by religious and political factions.
©Archivo Iconografico, S.A./Corbis. Reproduced by permission.

of Damascus was the Seljuk empire (see "The Arrival of the Seljuk Turks" in Chapter 4). To the southwest, around the southeastern coast of the Mediterranean Sea, was Muslim Egypt. Furthermore, the Byzantines (the Christians of the East), who felt betrayed by the Latin Christians (Christians of Europe), showed little interest in aiding their cause. And yet the Crusaders remained in control of the Crusader states without facing a major threat until the 1130s.

The Crusaders were able to do so primarily because they encountered little organized opposition. Both within the Crusader states and in the surrounding regions, Muslims were sharply divided by religious and political factions, or subgroups. The Egyptian Muslims hated the Turks while frequently trying to find a way to get along with the Christians. Many Arabs in the region claimed to be allied (on the same side) with the Egyptians. But these Arabs, especially those in rich seaport towns along the coast, were often more interested in retaining power locally than in maintaining allegiance, or loyalty, to a distant monarchy. The Turks, too, were divided, with the Seljuks contending with a rival clan called the Danishmends.

Even the Seljuks, who had seized large portions of the Byzantine Empire, were divided. Factions of the Seljuks were led by warlords who plotted and schemed to gain advantage over one another. These warlords included such figures as Duqaq in Damascus and Kerbogha in the city of Mosul. A third, Ridwan in the city of Aleppo, tried to cooperate with the Franks, earning the hatred of his Arab subjects. These divisions prevented the Arabs from mounting any kind of campaign to drive the Crusaders out of the Middle East. They were too occupied fighting among themselves both for political power and for control of their faith.

The emergence of the Shiite Muslims

The Muslim empire had grown steadily from the seventh through the tenth centuries, after the founding of Islam. Although Islam had many successes and converted many members to the faith, it faced a constant threat from within. The threat extended back almost to the founding of Islam. It arose over the question of who would succeed Muhammad as leader of the faith. When Muhammad died in 632, he left no instructions about who would follow him. An assembly of Muslim leaders in the city of Mecca (in modern-day Saudi Arabia), Muhammad's birthplace, chose a man named Abu Bakr as the first caliph, the term used to denote Muhammad's successor. Abu Bakr was one of Muhammad's closest associates and the father of Muhammad's second wife.

Immediately, a group formed that opposed the appointment of Abu Bakr. Members of this group believed that Muhammad's successor had to be a blood descendant from the Prophet, as Muhammad was called. They favored a man named Hazrat Ali ibn Abi Talib, or Ali, who was Muhammad's cousin and the husband of Muhammad's daughter Fatima. This dissident, or rebel, group became known as the Shi'at Ali, or "party of Ali," from which the name Shiite (often spelled Shi'ite) comes.

The Shiites were always a minority sect, or subgroup; by the early twenty-first century they made up perhaps a tenth of Muslims in the region. The main group of Muslims is called Sunni, a name meaning "orthodox." "Sunni" comes from the word *Sunna,* or "traditions," referring to writings that describe how Muhammad and his close associates dealt with certain issues. Even in the early years of the twenty-first century, tensions continued to divide the Sunnis and the Shiites in the Middle East.

The Umayyad dynasty

What followed was a long period of strife in Islam. Abu Bakr, the first caliph, named as his successor Umar. Abu Bakr and Umar had led an army against the Byzantine Empire and achieved a major victory over Byzantine forces in a battle at the Yarmuk River near the Sea of Galilee in 636. Umar, the second caliph, then seized Jerusalem after a lengthy siege in 638. Umar was murdered in 644 by a non-Muslim, and a power struggle developed among several men he had favored to succeed him. Out of this struggle, a man named Uthman became the third caliph.

Uthman came from a powerful, aristocratic Meccan clan called the Umayyads, so the family that led Islam now was called the Umayyad dynasty. The Umayyads moved the capital city of Islam from Mecca to Damascus in Syria. Because of Uthman's aristocratic background, Shiite resentment toward him became even greater. In 656 he was murdered by Muslim dissidents who continued to favor Ali, who came from a humbler background.

Ali thus finally became the fourth caliph, but following a civil war that did not resolve any disputes, he was murdered in 661, again by Muslim dissidents. With Ali gone, the Umayyad clan regained control of the faith, ruling the empire

Shiite Muslims and Karbala

The site of the Battle of Karbala is still a holy shrine for Shiite Muslims. They believe that Hussain deliberately sacrificed himself at Karbala for the Shiite sect of Islam. He wanted to be brutalized, or ill-treated, by the Umayyad caliph because he sought to demonstrate that rulers who governed by military force rather than by the word of Allah were evil. For this reason, Hussain's martyrdom, or death for the faith, is still celebrated by Shiites.

Hussain's martyrdom is commemorated on a religious holiday called Ashura. On this holiday, Shiite men hit themselves in the forehead until they bleed. The martyrdom of Hussain had great significance for the Shiites. The Shiite movement began and was justified because, in the view of the Shiites, Ali was denied his proper place as the first caliph after Muhammad died. His martyrdom, though, fueled the Shiite movement and, as Moojan Momen writes in *An Introduction to Shi'i Islam,* "implanted its ideas deep in the heart of the people." The Shiites remain an oppressed minority of Islam. They tend to be poorer and less educated than the Sunni majority.

from Damascus. Over the following decades the Umayyads conquered most of North Africa, overran much of Spain, and even marched into France, where they were stopped by the French king Charles Martel at the Battle of Tours in 732.

The division of Islam, though, was complete. The followers of Ali, the Shiites, condemned the Sunni Umayyads as illegitimate, believing that they were corrupt, or dishonest, and unfaithful to the teachings of the Prophet (Muhammad). The Shiite party reflected a great deal of unrest, particularly the resentment of non-Arab Muslims of the strong influence that Arabs had over the faith. In 680 Ali's youngest son, the Prophet's grandson Hussain ibn Ali (often spelled Hussein or Husayn), led the Shiites in another civil war against the Umayyads. The war ended when he and his family were killed in a historic battle at Karbala, south of Baghdad.

The Abbasid dynasty

Ali's death did not end civil war in the years that followed. The Sunnis from Damascus continued to offend other

A mausoleum of the Abbasid caliphs. This faction of Islam was descended from the prophet Muhammad's uncle, named Abbas. *©Charles and Josette Lenars/Corbis. Reproduced by permission.*

factions within Islam as they became more secularized—that is, as they separated religion from the affairs of state. In response, another rebel group formed. Members of this group were descendants of Muhammad's uncle, named Abbas, so they were called the Abbasids.

The Abbasids launched another civil war in 750. They captured Damascus and massacred the Umayyad caliph and

his family. They then moved the Islamic capital to Baghdad, the capital city of modern-day Iraq but at that time in the nation of Persia. From Baghdad, the Abbasid caliphate (the term used to refer to the office of caliph and his domains) ruled over the Muslim empire, which included Syria and Palestine (the nation in which Jerusalem was located), until 1258. The caliph, though, was something of a figurehead; that is, he did not wield much power. While the Baghdad caliphate provided the administrators and religious leaders, power was in the hands of the warriors, the Seljuk Turks. The Turks were Sunnis who were led by a sultan (the king of a Muslim state) in Isfahan, Iran.

Meanwhile, the only member of the Umayyad family to escape the massacre in Damascus—Abdurrahman—established an independent caliphate in Córdoba, Spain, in 755 (see "Spanish Islam" in Chapter 1). Because of the presence of an Islamic caliphate within its borders, European Chris-

A Muslim cemetery and mosque wall in Tunisia, the ancient stronghold of the Fatimid Shiite Muslims. This faction of Islam was descended from the prophet Muhammad's daughter Fatima. *©K.M. Westermann/Corbis. Reproduced by permission.*

tians began to see Islam as a growing threat. This feeling of being threatened eventually led to popular support for the Crusades. Other independent caliphates were formed in Morocco in 788, Tunisia in 800, and eastern Persia in 820. In 868 an independent caliphate was formed in Egypt, where the ruling Shiite family was called the Fatimid dynasty, named after Muhammad's daughter Fatima.

This division of Islam into factions, born of a complex and chaotic history, weakened Islam, although the Islamic empire was rich in trade, agriculture, manufacturing, commerce, and learning; Damascus, for example, had seventy libraries. Divisions, though, prevented Islam from presenting a united front against the Crusaders. The movement of the capital from Damascus, which lay just to the east of the Crusader states, to the more distant city of Baghdad would prove fateful. The greater distance from Palestine made it harder for the caliphate to lead opposition to the Crusaders. For their part, the Crusaders were able to take advantage of this factionalism, or division. Often aiding one side and then another, they kept the Muslims on their toes, focused on one another rather than on ridding their lands of the colonists. In fact, at times it was in the interest of one Muslim faction or another to aid the Europeans.

An example concerns the formation of a fourth Crusader state, the County of Tripoli, which lay between Jerusalem and the two Crusader states to the north, Edessa and Antioch. The Muslim emir, or ruler, of Tripoli, learned that forces from Damascus were planning to ambush Baldwin, who was on the march with a small Crusader force from Edessa to Jerusalem to assume the throne of the kingdom after his brother, Godfrey, died. The emir of Tripoli wanted to retain control over the city for himself and did not want Damascus to meddle in Tripoli, so he tipped off Baldwin, allowing him to escape the ambush. Then later, in 1109, when Raymond of Toulouse and a small band of Christian knights marched on Tripoli, Damascus got its revenge on the emir when the forces it sent to help defend the city refused to fight. Only in this way did Tripoli fall and become a fourth Crusader state. A unified Islamic response in Tripoli probably would have prevented the city from falling to the Christians. Without Tripoli, the Crusader states in the north would have remained cut off from Jerusalem.

The Assassins

Another example of the divisions that undermined Islam in responding to the Crusaders was the formation of a Shiite group called the Assassins. The name was invented by the West; members of the Assassins would have referred to themselves as Ismailis. This name refers to an imam, or Shiite Muslim religious leader, named Ismail, who the group believed was divine. Assassins, then and in the twenty-first century, carry out planned murders for religious or political purposes. One theory about the source of the name is that it comes from the word *hashish,* the drug that members of the group used when they carried out their missions.

The Assassins dedicated themselves to overthrowing the Sunnis and returning Islam to what they considered the true path of the faith. The most militant, or aggressive, wing of the Assassins was formed in about 1090, just five years before Pope Urban II called the First Crusade, by a learned man

A painting depicting the taking of Tripoli. Tripoli became the fourth Crusader state and was important because it allowed the Crusader states to the north access to Jerusalem. *Chateau de Versailles, France/ Giraudon/Bridgman Art Library. Reproduced by permission.*

A set of doors with intricate metalwork in a mosque found in Cairo, Egypt. Even though most of Egypt was Muslim, there was constant fighting between the Sunni and Shiite factions. *©Dave Bartruff/Corbis. Reproduced by permission.*

named Hasan al-Sabah. His original goal was to base his movement in Shiite Egypt, from there assassinating Sunni leaders. But the Egyptian caliph had no desire to harbor a band of terrorists, so Hasan and his group were forced underground. In the years that followed, they tried to disrupt Sunni Islam wherever they could. For example, in Syria they fanned the flames of disagreement between the Sunni emirs. Thus the Assassins not only became outcasts and sworn enemies of Sunni Islam, but they also became the enemies of the Shiite caliphate in Egypt. For this reason, Hasan actively worked on many occasions for the benefit of the Crusaders, his only ally in defeating Sunni Islam.

Jihad

None of this is to say that Islam mounted no opposition to the Franks. In the years after the First Crusade and the capture by Christians of Jerusalem, some Muslims revived the tradition of *jihad,* usually translated as "holy war." The concept of a holy war for Islam was first developed in the seventh century, when Muslims fought the Byzantine Empire to gain control of Jerusalem. Many of those who fought against the Byzantines had been given grants of land, which had remained in the same families for more than four centuries. Now those lands were being lost to the Christians, and some Muslims wanted to fight back.

Thus *jihad* reemerged in the early years of the twelfth century, after the Crusaders seized Tripoli in 1109, then the cities of Beirut and Sidon in 1110. Many desperate Muslims fled these cities, taking refuge in Damascus and Aleppo, both cities in Syria. They were looking for some way to oppose what was happening in their land. In Aleppo an influential judge named Abu al-Fadl ibn al-Khashshab tried to persuade the Turkish ruler to call on the Baghdad caliphate for help in driving out the Christians. The Turkish ruler, Ridwan, though, was trying to get along with the Christians, so al-Khashshab went to Baghdad himself in early 1111.

Military power in Baghdad lay with the Turks, not the Arabs. The Turks supported al-Khashshab, because they wanted to assert their authority over Aleppo. Accordingly, the Turkish sultan ordered his army to get ready for "Holy War against the infidel [unbeliever, in this case the Christians] enemies of God." In this way, *jihad* was launched against the Christians.

Even so, little damage was done to the Christians. The Turkish sultan sent his force to Aleppo, but in the meantime Ridwan had arrested al-Khashshab and barricaded the city. He believed that the Turks were coming not to "rescue" him but to seize control of the city. After the Turkish forces arrived, they vandalized the area around Aleppo but then left without taking the city. While nothing was done about Christians in Syria and Palestine, the seeds of holy war had been planted.

For More Information

Books

Chambers, Mortimer, et al. *The Western Experience,* 8th ed. New York: McGraw-Hill, 2003.

Lewis, Bernard, ed. *Islam: From the Prophet Muhammad to the Capture of Constantinople.* Vol. 1, *Politics and War.* Vol. 2, *Religion and Society.* New York: Oxford University Press, 1987.

Momen, Moojan. *An Introduction to Shi'i Islam: The History and Doctrines of Twelve Shi'ism.* New Haven, CT: Yale University Press, 1987.

Von Grunebaum, Gustave E., ed. *Medieval Islam: A Study in Cultural Orientation.* Chicago: University of Chicago Press, 1971.

History of the Crusades

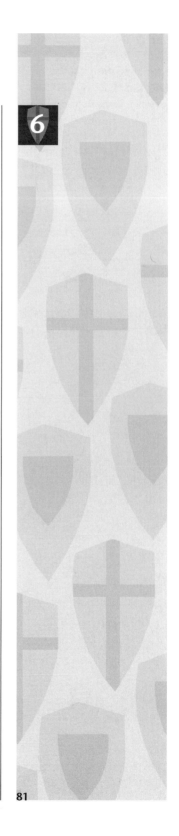

6

The word "crusade" emerged from the Romance languages of Europe, especially French and Spanish, during the Middle Ages—the era in Europe roughly from the years 500 to 1500, often called the medieval period. (These languages are called Romance languages not because they are "romantic" but because they evolved from southern Europe and the region around Rome.) The Old French word *crois* and the Spanish *cruz* mean "cross." From these words came the French *croisée* and the Spanish *cruzada*. Both of these words mean something like "to take up the cross," and the connotation (intended significance) of both was that the cross was that on which Christ was crucified. The English word "crusade" developed from these words.

That is "crusade" with a small "c." With a capital "C," the term "Crusades" has a more specific meaning. Historians use it to refer to the series of military campaigns launched by the Christian countries of western Europe beginning in the late eleventh century. During these campaigns tens of thousands of men, and even some women, "took up the cross" for the church. As a sign of their vow to their faith, they pledged to wear a large Christian

cross embroidered on their armor and shields. Their goal was to recapture Palestine from the hands of the Muslims and restore it to Christian control. The chief focus of the Crusaders was the Holy City of Jerusalem (see Chapter 2 on the Holy City of Jerusalem), but the impact of the Crusades was felt throughout that region of the world as well as throughout Europe.

Historians conventionally number the Crusades. The First Crusade was launched in late 1095 and ended with the capture of Jerusalem in 1099. The last, or the Seventh, Crusade ended in 1250, although the Crusader presence in the region did not end until the fall of the last Christian outpost, Acre, in 1291. Historians identify seven separate Crusades, but the Crusades were a single extended conflict that was fought in waves or stages over nearly two centuries.

The sermon at Clermont

Pope Urban II's first step after receiving the Byzantine emperor Alexius's appeal for help in liberating the Holy Land (see "A Cry for Help" in Chapter 4) was to plan a church council in Clermont, a city in the south-central French province of Auvergne. The council took place in November 1095. Late in the day on November 27, a crowd began to assemble in a field outside Clermont. Many of those in the crowd were bishops, barons (noblemen), and Frankish knights (that is, knights from the Frankish empire, or France). Many others were simple townsfolk and people from the surrounding countryside.

The pope ascended a large elevated platform and began to preach a sermon. Playing expertly on his listeners' emotions, Urban told them about bloodshed in the East, about atrocities (acts of violence) committed by Muslims against Christians. He inflamed his audience by pointing out that these evils were committed not only against Eastern Orthodox Christians (members of the eastern branch of Christianity) but also against pilgrims from the West who were visiting the Holy Land. He painted a picture of the holy city of Jerusalem in the hands of infidels (unbelievers), who were desecrating, or violating and damaging, places sacred to all Christians. Most important, he called on his listeners, especially the Frankish knights, to come to the aid of their Christian brothers and free the city of Jerusalem, including the tomb of Christ, from the infidel. The crowd responded enthusiastically, chanting "God wills it!" The knights and nobles fell to their knees. They proclaimed their allegiance to the pope and vowed to fight in his holy cause. "God wills it!" became a battle cry during the Crusades.

On that chilly afternoon in Clermont, the First Crusade began. For the next nine months, Urban traveled across

France, preaching the Crusade. His appeal met with overwhelming popular approval. All through Europe—but especially in France, Germany, and Italy—priests, monks, and bishops signed up recruits, who saw in the pope's appeal a chance to win salvation for their souls. A kind of religious frenzy affected many people of Europe. Warfare came to be seen as a way to serve God.

The First Crusade

From August through October 1096 groups of trained troops, each under the command of a noble, departed from Europe. Most were from France, although significant numbers were from Germany and Italy. The first group, under the command of a noble named Hugh of Vermandois, arrived at Constantinople in October. This group was followed by others through the winter and into the spring of 1097, including those led by the brothers Godfrey, Eustace, and Baldwin from France and a contingent from Italy led by Bohemond of Taranto.

The road to Jerusalem

The relationship between the western knights and the Byzantines was tense. The Byzantines had already had to deal with the People's Crusade (see "Religious Hysteria" in Chapter 4) and were inclined to think of the westerners as crude, ignorant barbarians. For their part, the western knights regarded the Byzantines as soft. Despite these tensions, the European and Byzantine forces cooperated, at least for a while. The combined army of Crusaders and Greeks, numbering perhaps sixty thousand, stood assembled at the extreme western edge of Asia Minor in Anatolia (a region in western Turkey). Its first objective was Nicaea, a strategically valuable city located just across the Bosphorus Strait from Constantinople. Nicaea was a Turkish sultanate (a region or country ruled by a Muslim sultan, or king) under the command of Kilij Arslan. Arslan was the commander who had destroyed the People's Crusade.

The Crusaders suffered heavy casualties in a battle with Arslan's forces, but their formations held, and the Turks had to withdraw. In May the Crusaders and Byzantines laid siege to Nicaea, which surrendered to Alexius on June 19,

1097. Flushed with success, the Crusaders, now about 700 miles (1,127 kilometers) from the Holy Land and expecting to get there in six weeks, turned their attention to the next city on the route, Dorylaeum. Arslan, though, had different ideas and planned an ambush along their way. Again, despite heavy losses, the Crusader formations held, and the Turks withdrew. The road to Jerusalem seemed clear.

The siege of Antioch

The Crusaders set out for Antioch, a city on the eastern shore of the Mediterranean Sea. Antioch was a large city that controlled the overland route into Syria and thus to Jerusalem, so it was a key objective for the Crusaders.

The Crusaders arrived at Antioch in October and laid siege to the heavily fortified city. (To "lay siege" means to surround a fortified city or castle, cut off supplies from the outside, and hope to starve those inside into surrendering.) The task was daunting, for the city was surrounded by 25 miles (40 kilometers) of walls and 400 towers. As weeks turned into months, the Crusaders ran out of money and food. Many of the poorer Crusaders died of starvation. Convinced that the situation was hopeless, the few Byzantine troops who had remained with the Crusaders returned to Constantinople. Many of the Crusaders deserted, often fleeing under cover of night. On June 3, 1098, after seven months, the siege finally succeeded after Bohemond discovered a corrupt, discontented guard who secretly admitted the Crusaders to the city.

The miracle at Antioch

Word had reached the Crusaders that a massive Turkish army was approaching Antioch to come to its defense. The situation seemed desperate. After seven months of siege, little food was left in the city. The Crusaders, now themselves trapped inside the city's walls, were nearly delirious with starvation and despair.

When matters stood at their most desperate, a common foot soldier by the name of Peter Bartholomew met with Raymond of Toulouse, one of the leaders of the First Crusade, and Pope Urban's representative, the bishop of Le Puy, and claimed that he had had a vision in which Saint An-

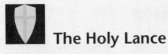

The Holy Lance

The discovery of the Holy Lance in Antioch during the First Crusade was almost certainly a hoax. What may be the true lance has been in the hands of various leaders, including the Roman emperor Constantine; Charlemagne ("Charles the Great"), the legendary Frankish king of the late eighth and early ninth centuries; the French emperor Napoleon in the nineteenth century; and the German Nazi dictator Adolf Hitler in the twentieth century. These and other rulers believed that the lance was a source of mystical power. After World War II (1939–45), American forces located the lance and returned it to a museum in Vienna, Austria, where it is housed today. Experts using the tools of modern science continue to investigate whether it could indeed be the actual lance that pierced Christ's side.

drew revealed to him the location of the Holy Lance. This was the lance that a Roman soldier named Longinus had used to pierce Christ's side as he hung on the cross—and it was buried, said Peter, under Saint Peter's Cathedral in Antioch. Raymond was doubtful, but on June 15 he ordered his men to excavate, or dig, under the cathedral. Nothing was found until Peter leaped into the pit and emerged with an iron lance. The Crusaders, inspired by their belief that the Holy Lance had been found, recovered their strength and were ready to do battle against the Turks.

Events took an even stranger twist as the Crusaders marched out of the city behind the Holy Lance and priests bearing crosses. As they approached the Turkish army, all on white horses and carrying white banners, the Turks mysteriously turned and fled. To the weakened eyes of the starving Crusaders, they seemed almost to melt away, like ghosts. The Crusaders believed that God looked on their cause with favor and had come to their aid with a miracle. The reality, though, was that many of the Turkish troops suspected that their commander was fighting not to defend Islam but to seize land for himself. So at the critical moment, they decided simply not to fight and withdrew from the field.

Onward to the holy city

Bohemond and Raymond quarreled over who was going to take charge of Antioch. Bohemond wanted it for himself, but Raymond remained true to his oath to Alexius and insisted that the city be turned over to the Byzantines. Food was still in short supply, and some of the Crusaders may have resorted to cannibalism (eating their comrades).

Perhaps the most ironic turn of events was that the Fatimids, the Egyptian Muslim dynasty that had controlled Jerusalem since 638, had regained control of the city the previous year. This was a key event, for it undermined the very foundation of the Crusades. With the Fatimids back in control, the threat to Christian pilgrims from the Seljuks, the Turkish Muslim clan that had overrun Palestine and seized Jerusalem, no longer existed. Christians again had ready access to the holy city.

The Crusades should have ended with the capture of Antioch, but a kind of unreason had taken hold of the remaining Crusaders. They had lived with their dream for so long that they could not give it up. They were driven by a passion for what they believed was a holy cause; a need to fulfill their Crusader vows; and a lust for Muslim blood, the spoils of war, and territory.

Over the next six months the Crusaders made their way south toward Jerusalem, now just 300 miles (483 kilometers) away. They met with little resistance along the way. Further quarrels erupted over who among the Crusaders would take control of such cities as Tripoli and Arqa. Finally, though, the Crusaders—about twenty thousand survivors—mounted a hill called Montjoie. They reached the top of the hill, and before them lay their goal. After three years of hardship and toil, of disease, thirst, hunger, and death, they set up their camps outside the holy city of Jerusalem. The date was June 7, 1099.

The siege of Jerusalem

The Egyptian sultan in control of Jerusalem was not overly concerned by the arrival of the Crusaders. Just the year before, he had taken the city from the Turks. He had at his command forty catapults that could rain death and destruction on anyone who tried to breach the city's walls (see "Siege Warfare" in Chapter 10). He knew that the Crusaders did not have any siege machinery of their own and that they could not build any, for he had ordered every tree within miles cut down. He also knew that they had little food and almost no water—because he had had all the wells outside the city poisoned. He was concerned about the lack of manpower at his command, but Egypt promised to send more troops by the end of July if he could hold out until then.

Once again, a seeming miracle gave a boost to the Crusaders. One day, a Norman knight named Tancred was leading an expedition searching for food and supplies when he happened across the mouth of a cave. Inside, to his astonishment, he found four hundred large abandoned timbers. The Crusaders quickly gathered the timbers and began to assemble towers for scaling the walls. Morale flagged under the searing heat of the summer, but it again was boosted when the priests led a barefoot procession around the city as the Crusaders sang and blew trumpets. The scorn and insults heaped down by the Muslims from the top of the city walls steeled the resolve (determination) of the Crusaders, who completed the towers just five days later.

On the night of July 14, 1099, the Crusaders began to move the towers into place, often while ducking arrows and firebombs from above. On the morning of July 15, Godfrey and his men had their tower in place against the north wall of the city. By noon they had constructed a bridge to the top of the wall. The first Crusaders leaped across and entered the city. They and their men opened the gates of the city, and the Crusaders rushed inside.

The massacre

What followed cannot be explained. Certain it is, though, that the Crusaders abandoned any adherence to the knight's code of chivalry, or gallantry (see Chapter 9 on knights and the traditions of chivalry). As they stormed the city, they were overtaken by sheer blood lust. They rampaged through the city, killing everyone in sight, including women and children. As many as twenty thousand people lay dead at the end of the invasion. They stormed al-Aqsa Mosque and slaughtered the Muslims who had taken refuge there. They set fire to the synagogue (Jewish house of worship) in which the city's Jews had taken refuge. They seized homes and any personal property on which they could lay their hands. Within days the stench of dead bodies had become so great that the few surviving Muslims were ordered to pile the bodies outside the city walls, where they were burned. It was God's will, the Crusaders believed, that they cleanse the holy city of unbelievers. When their thirst for blood was satisfied, they gathered in the Church of the Holy Sepulchre to pray.

The Kingdom of Jerusalem

The first task that lay before the Crusaders was to establish a purely Latin Christian kingdom in Jerusalem and the surrounding area. They elected Godfrey as the city's ruler, but Godfrey declined to take the title of king, saying that he could not wear a crown in the city where Christ had been forced to wear a crown of thorns during his Crucifixion. He took instead the title Defender (or sometimes Advocate) of the Holy Sepulchre. In this role he was to rule over what the French came to call Outremer, meaning "the land overseas." Outremer encompassed not only Jerusalem but also the other cities the Crusaders had captured. These Crusader states included the kingdoms of Antioch, Edessa, and later Tripoli— all under the authority of Jerusalem.

The second task was to deal with the Egyptian army that Cairo had sent but that had not arrived in time to save Jerusalem. This army, which greatly outnumbered that of the Crusaders, camped at the nearby town of Ascalon. Before the Egyptians could begin an assault, the Crusaders marched out and launched a surprise attack at sunrise on August 12. They decisively defeated the Egyptians, putting an end to any further Muslim resistance.

Godfrey died just a year later, and the kingship went to his brother Baldwin, who was crowned king of Jerusalem on Christmas Day 1100. By this time, most of the Crusaders had returned home. As time went on, many who remained in the East adopted Middle Eastern dress and customs. Some even learned to speak bits of the Arabic language. The Europeans and their descendants began to establish business relationships and occasionally even personal friendships with the Jews, Greeks, and Muslims in the area. They undertook a massive building and renovation program (see Chapter 2 about the Holy City of Jerusalem). A French writer named Fulcher of Chartres, who chronicled the early years of the Crusades, wrote in *A History of the Expedition to Jerusalem, 1095–1127*: "We who were Occidentals [westerners] have now become Orientals. He who was a Roman or a Frank has in this land been made into a Galilean or a Palestinian.... We

Baldwin I crossing the River Jordan. Baldwin was crowned king of Jerusalem on Christmas Day 1100.
Bibliotheque Nationale, Paris, France/Giraudon/Bridgeman Art Library. Reproduced by permission.

have already forgotten the places of our birth.... He who was born an alien has become as a native."

In time, an air of normality settled over the area, although Jerusalem and the other kingdoms were weakened by infighting. This state of affairs would last for about four decades. Then, in a development that startled all of Europe, Edessa fell to a Muslim Turk.

The Second Crusade

The few thousand Europeans who remained in Jerusalem and the other Crusader states—Antioch, Edessa, and Tripoli—knew that they were vulnerable to attack. But for nearly four decades, no one seemed prepared to step forward and lead the Muslims in an effort to expel the colonists from their land. Inspiration finally came from a Turkish leader named Imad al-Din Zengi, who in 1137 struck with full force at Tripoli, besieged the Frankish garrison (occupying force) that had taken refuge in a nearby castle, and gained control of the city.

In 1144 Zengi set his sights on Edessa, which was the weakest of the Christian kingdoms because of political infighting and a lack of manpower. He besieged Edessa for four weeks, finally entering on Christmas Eve after his men dug tunnels beneath the city's massive walls and set the timbers supporting the walls on fire. In a scene reminiscent of that in Jerusalem forty-five years earlier, Zengi's men slaughtered thousands of men, women, and children. Zengi, though, made it clear that his goal was to drive out the Franks. He ordered that the city's native Eastern Orthodox Christians be spared.

News of Zengi's triumph spread throughout Europe and the Middle East. This was the first time that the Muslims had reclaimed a city from the Franks. It inspired Muslims and terrified leaders both in the West and in Jerusalem. Jerusalem appealed to Europe and the pope for help. The driving force behind the Second Crusade was a monk named Bernard, the abbot of the monastery at Clairvaux in France. Bernard was known throughout Europe as a charismatic (magnetic and captivating) and persuasive speaker. Wherever he went, massive crowds gathered to hear him. Bernard believed that the fall of Edessa was a blessing in disguise. It would give a new generation of Crusaders an opportunity to win salvation by rescuing the Holy Land.

Bernard launched the Second Crusade on March 31, 1146. In a field outside Vézelay, France, he mounted a platform and delivered a stirring Crusade sermon. The large crowd was fired with enthusiasm, mobbing the platform to take the cross. Before long, two massive armies were assembled. The first, led by Conrad III, the emperor of the Holy Roman Empire, departed for the Holy Land in May 1146. The other, led by Louis VII of France, left in June. Their journey was not easy. When Conrad's Germans reached the area around Nicaea, Kilij Arslan's son attacked, wanting to avenge his father's defeat on nearly the same spot a half century earlier. By this time, the Germans were tired and desperately thirsty, and in the short battle that followed nearly nine out of ten soldiers lost their lives.

The remnants of the German army escaped to Nicaea. There they met up with the Franks, who themselves had suffered

Louis VII of France, Emperor Conrad III of Germany, and King Baldwin III of Jerusalem deliberating the course of the Second Crusade. *©Bettmann/Corbis. Reproduced by permission.*

heavy losses at the hands of the Turks as they crossed Asia Minor. The combined forces then started to make their way to Jerusalem.

The fiasco at Damascus

The Second Crusade was a military and political disaster. Eager to engage the Muslims, any Muslims, the Crusaders turned on Damascus in Syria. Their goal was to strengthen the eastern borders of the Crusader states by seizing control of the city. This was a blunder so monumental that it has no explanation. Damascus itself had recently been threatened by Zengi's forces. It was the Christians' only Muslim ally. For its own protection, it had actually formed an alliance with Jerusalem to repel Zengi. By attacking Damascus, the Crusaders foolishly managed to make an enemy of the one Muslim city in the region that was inclined to be friendly toward the Franks.

The Crusaders left Jerusalem for Damascus on May 25, 1148. As the Christian army approached the city, the betrayed

Muslim leaders there made an appeal to Zengi's son, Nur al-Din, a zealous proponent of *jihad,* or holy war, against the Christians. Even though al-Din himself had been threatening Damascus, the ruler of the city concluded that his only choice was to try to join forces with al-Din to drive off the Crusaders (see "Zengi, Nur al-Din, and Saladin" in Chapter 7).

Oddly, the chief protection that Damascus enjoyed was provided not by harsh terrain or other natural barriers but by groves of fruit trees. These groves stretched for up to 5 miles (8 kilometers) away from the city. The trees were planted close together, and each grove was enclosed by high walls of mud. The Crusaders were picked off singly or in small groups by archers on towers in the middle of the groves or foot soldiers armed with lances lurking behind the walls. The Crusaders persisted, though, and drove the Damascenes back behind the city walls.

Then the Crusaders committed a second blunder. Rather than holding the groves, they suddenly moved their

An illustration of the siege of Damascus during the Second Crusade. The print shows the armies of King Baldwin III of Jerusalem (upper left), Emperor Conrad III of Germany (right), and King Louis VII of France (lower left). *Reproduced by permission of The British Library (Royal 15 E. I).*

forces to an open plain east of the city. The Damascenes, by now reinforced with refugees and soldiers pouring in from the north, retook the groves. Meanwhile, the Crusaders quickly discovered that there was no water on the plain.

At this point, under the merciless heat of the summer sun, they concluded that the odds of winning were bleak. So they packed up and began a humiliating retreat to Jerusalem. In all, the fighting had lasted about a week. Thus ended the Second Crusade, in stark contrast to the First Crusade. The Crusaders had succeeded only in weakening the Christian kingdoms, making an enemy of Damascus, and strengthening al-Din, who continued to march against Frankish territory in the Middle East.

The Christian response

Nur al-Din continued to nibble at Frankish territory, but he became preoccupied with fighting the Egyptian Muslims. Egypt was wealthy, but its politics were chaotic. The Crusaders were ready to take advantage of this weakness in the Egyptian dynasty. They turned their attention southward to Ascalon, a city that stood between the kingdom of Jerusalem and Egypt and the only city along the Mediterranean coast that had never fallen to the Franks. In 1153 the Crusaders launched a four-month siege of the city, which finally fell in July. The capture of Ascalon was a great triumph, the last one the Crusaders would ever know. For the next century after the capture of Ascalon, the history of the Crusades, from a western perspective, would be a story largely of defeat.

Meanwhile, al-Din was gaining his own triumphs. Damascus fell to his forces without a fight in April 1154. Suddenly, he found himself commander of a large strip of territory on the eastern border of the remaining Crusader states. He might have been the one who drove the Franks out of Muslim lands, but once again he became preoccupied with fighting the Turks to the north and then Egypt. By this time he was growing old and frail. Rather than leading troops in the field, he was spending most of his time in Damascus. He turned his authority over to his successor, Saladin. Saladin proved to be the most fearsome Muslim warrior the Crusaders ever faced. It was to counter Saladin that the Third Crusade was called.

The Third Crusade

Saladin is the common name given to Salah al-Din Yusuf (1137–1193), who by this time had surrounded the Crusader states as sultan of Syria and Egypt. During the Third Crusade and the centuries that followed, his was perhaps the one name of a Muslim warrior that became widely known in other parts of the world, inspiring a mixture of fear and respect.

The fall of Jerusalem

The Crusaders were in disarray throughout these years, roughly the 1170s and early 1180s. Internal divisions, infighting, and disputes over succession to the throne of Jerusalem weakened the Crusader states. At one point, civil war threatened the Kingdom of Jerusalem. Only one thing could hold the Kingdom together: an attack by Saladin, which would require the factions, or divided groups, to put aside their differences to preserve the kingdom. But at this point, a state of truce existed between Jerusalem and Saladin. The only thing to do, then, was to break the truce and provoke Saladin. This task fell to the Christian ruler of Antioch, a corrupt man named Reynald of Châtillon. After Reynald attacked a Muslim caravan, Saladin assembled an army of about thirty thousand regular troops and a large number of volunteers and declared war on the Crusaders.

Saladin struck first on July 1, 1187, at the town of Tiberias, located near the Sea of Galilee. Meanwhile, the king of Jerusalem, having learned of Saladin's intentions, had gathered his forces to come to the city's defense and was already on the march. On July 3 they made camp in the desert near the Horns of Hattin, two hills outside Tiberias. On the night of July 3, Saladin's men encircled the camp and set fire to all of the surrounding brush. The following morning, they attacked. Desperately thirsty and with smoke in their eyes, the Franks could put up little resistance, and most were killed or fled.

Saladin's victory at the Battle of Hattin was a turning point in the history of the Crusades. Saladin had just wiped out almost the entire army of Jerusalem, which now stood unprotected to the southwest. Meeting little resistance, he seized nearly every town along the route to the holy city, except for Tripoli, Antioch, and Tyre. Jerusalem fell without a

Saladin

King Guy and Reynald of Châtillon were both taken prisoner and delivered to Saladin at his tent after the Battle of Hattin. There, Saladin behaved in a way that contributed to his reputation. Gracious in victory, he offered the parched king a drink of water, which Guy gratefully accepted. When Guy tried to offer the goblet to Reynald, Saladin stopped him. Having extended refreshment to Guy, Saladin, by the rules of Arabic hospitality, was obligated to offer him personal protection. But Saladin had no inclination to offer the same protection to the treacherous Reynald. Reynald was taken from the tent, where, moments later, Saladin drew his sword and beheaded him. This type of act was typical of Saladin, who could be noble and generous one moment, and rash and violent the next.

fight on October 2, 1187. In contrast to the scene nearly nine decades earlier in the holy city, no massacre took place, although many of the city's Christians were sold into slavery.

Once again, western Christians were shocked by news from the Levant (the countries on the eastern shore of the Mediterranean). Pope Gregory VIII called for a Third Crusade, which met with an enthusiastic response from the people of Europe. Even before a Crusade was organized, volunteers were arriving by boat in Tyre and Tripoli from England, Flanders, France, Germany, Hungary, and Denmark.

The first organized European force left for the Holy Land on May 11, 1189. It was led by Frederick Barbarossa ("Red Beard"), the Holy Roman Emperor, who believed that the Third Crusade would be the pinnacle, or peak, of his long career as ruler of an empire that dominated central Europe. But once again, crossing Asia Minor proved to be a major stumbling block. The Germans were harassed continuously by the Turks, and they were dying by the thousands of hunger and thirst. When they arrived at the banks of a cool river in Asia Minor, Frederick could not resist plunging in, where he drowned. The German Crusade thus came to an abrupt end, as most of the remnants of Frederick's leaderless forces turned around and went home.

This left the Third Crusade in the hands of two other European kings, Philip II of France and the newly crowned Richard I of England. Richard was born at a time when France and England were almost constantly at war, largely because of England's occupation of western France. When he came of age, he was knighted by the French king Louis, and he actually learned the arts of war fighting against the forces of his own father. After ascending to the throne of England, Richard

German participation in the Third Crusade came to an abrupt end in 1190 after its leader Frederick I (also known as Frederick Barbarossa), drowned in the Goksu River pictured here. ©Ruggero Vanni/Corbis. Reproduced by permission.

was now in the odd position of having to turn and fight the French, because half of the country was part of his domain. But he had been raised in the French court, where he had learned to think of the English as backward bumpkins.

Popular support for the Crusade was demanding that Richard and Philip put aside their differences to fight Saladin. Each knew that if he left his country to join the Crusade, the

Richard, Saladin, and Chivalry

A number of legends grew up around Saladin and his willingness to extend the hand of chivalry (courtesy) to Richard. In one battle Richard's horse was killed. Saladin believed that a king, any king, should not have to suffer the indignity of fighting on foot, so he called a truce and had two horses delivered to the English king.

On another occasion, Richard fell ill with a fever. Saladin, not wanting to defeat any other than Europe's best, sent his personal physician to Richard, as well as gifts of fruit and even snow from the top of Mount Ascalon to cool him. The physician's potion apparently worked, and Richard returned to the field of battle.

These stories may or may not be true, but they became part of the legend of Saladin and his relationship with Richard. They made Saladin almost as much of a hero in the West as he was in the Middle East.

other would attack. The only choice the two kings had was to join forces to fight the common foe. To that end, they levied a special tax, called the "Saladin tithe" (tithe means "tenth" and refers to the custom of Christians of contributing a tenth of their income to the church), to finance what promised to be an expensive expedition.

The two kings met at Vézelay, France, where they assembled their armies. Rather than following the overland route that had defeated Frederick and others before him, they agreed to travel through southern Italy, Sicily, and Cyprus and arrive in the Holy Land by boat. By this time, Guy of Jerusalem had won his freedom from Saladin. He assembled a small army and joined the siege of the city of Acre, which had been going on for nearly two years as Christian forces tried to gain control of it from the Turks. Philip joined him first, followed by Richard, who landed at Acre on June 8, 1191.

Saladin hoped that quarrels would break out among the Crusaders, weakening their resolve. His hope was partially realized. After the city fell to the Crusaders on July 12, 1191, the question arose as to who was going to raise his banner over the city. At one point, Leopold, the duke of Austria, who commanded the handful of Frederick's troops still in the field, planted his banner in the city. Richard tore it down and threw it into a moat, an impulsive act he would come to regret later. Meanwhile, factions (dissenting groups) quarreled over who would rule the city.

At this point Philip, always more of a politician than a warrior, felt that he had done his duty to his church. After promising Richard that he would not attack western France, he returned home. He had been a reluctant Crusader from the start and took part only because he was pressured to do so by his nobles and popular opinion. The duke of Austria, as well as several other minor nobles from various European countries, also left, annoyed by Richard's impulsiveness and high-handedness. The Third Crusade was now entirely in the hands of Richard I, known as "the Lionheart."

Richard and Saladin

Richard departed for Jerusalem on August 22, 1191. He had trouble getting his forces to cooperate, for Acre was a lively city, and recently an entire boatload of prostitutes had arrived. Imposing tight discipline in the summer heat, he first approached the city of Arsuf, where Saladin launched an assault. Richard was able to maintain discipline, keep his troops in formation, and cut down the Muslim attackers. As a result, Saladin withdrew, badly beaten.

After the Battle of Arsuf, Richard easily took the near-by coastal city of Jaffa. He knew, though, that Jerusalem would be harder to capture. Further, he had received word that his brother John was causing unrest in England and that the country seemed headed toward civil war. Just as disturbing was news that Philip, going back on his word, was threatening to invade Normandy. Richard concluded that he needed to negotiate a peace treaty with Saladin.

Saladin responded by sending his brother, al-Malik al-Adil, to bargain with Richard. The terms of the treaty Richard proposed were extraordinary, and utterly at odds with the purpose of the Third Crusade, the recapture of Jerusalem. Under the treaty, al-Adil would marry Richard's sister Joanna. Joanna and al-Adil would jointly rule Jerusalem. Richard and Saladin would withdraw their forces and go home. Joanna, though, refused to marry a Muslim, and when al-Adil de-

A basin bearing the name of al-Malik al-Adil. Saladin had sent his brother, al-Adil, to negotiate a treaty with Richard I of England in order to end the Third Crusade. The treaty, however, never came to be. *Louvre, Paris, France/Lauros/Giraudon/Bridgeman Art Library. Reproduced by permission.*

clined to convert to Christianity, the negotiations broke down.

For his part, Saladin, too, needed a treaty. His defeat at Arsuf had tarnished his reputation for invincibility. His troops were exhausted. Many of the emirs (Muslim rulers) who had joined him were growing discontented, and even the ambitious al-Adil was giving indications that he was open to negotiations with Richard. Saladin's coalition, based on religious zeal and popular resentment of the Franks, seemed to be falling apart.

Accordingly, the two reached an agreement in March 1192. Under the terms of the treaty, Saladin would retain control over Jerusalem, with the provision that any Christian pilgrim would be allowed to visit the holy city. A piece of the Holy Cross on which Christ had been crucified, which was in Muslim possession in the city, would be turned over to the Franks. The Franks, in turn, retained a ribbon of territory along the coast extending from Tyre to Jaffa. Holding on to these cities was important, for Europeans could then still pursue their commercial interests in the Middle East.

Richard was about to go home and had returned to Acre to begin preparations when Saladin's army inexplicably attacked and recaptured Jaffa. Richard immediately boarded ship with what knights he could muster (gather) and set sail for Jaffa. Some days after he and his forces made camp outside the city, Saladin and his army attacked. Richard and his small army successfully repelled the attack against seemingly overwhelming odds. It was this battle, perhaps, that cemented Richard's reputation as a brave and heroic commander. Finally, on September 2, 1192, Richard and Saladin signed the treaty that had been negotiated in March. On October 9, Richard left the Holy Land for England.

The Third Crusade had a postscript. As he was returning home, Richard was shipwrecked and had to take the overland route. His journey took him through the domains of the duke of Austria, the same duke whose banner he had thrown into a moat at Acre. Richard tried to disguise himself, but he was recognized at an inn in Vienna. The duke seized him on a charge of murder and turned him over to the Holy Roman Emperor, who held him for ransom (payment for release). Richard remained a prisoner for a year and was released only after a huge ransom was paid.

Richard believed that the Third Crusade had been a success. He strengthened the Frankish hold on the coast and ensured Christians safe passage to the Holy Land. Pope Innocent III, though, took a different view. Richard had failed to reclaim the holy city of Jerusalem. Thus, in 1198 the pope called a new Crusade.

The Fourth Crusade

At the time of the Fourth Crusade, the Kingdom of Jerusalem was ruled by a court in exile at the port city of Acre. The kingdom the court ruled was a small strip of land, at its widest about 10 miles (16 kilometers), that ran from Jaffa to Tyre. This holding, along with Antioch and Tripoli, represented the tattered remnants of the original Crusader states.

Jerusalem, meanwhile, was under the control of Saladin's brother, al-Adil. On the throne in Rome at this time was Pope Innocent III, who believed that the pope, as God's representative on earth, should rule over God's entire earthly kingdom. He bullied and threatened the kings of Europe. He called for the submission of the Eastern Orthodox Church to Rome. And he became obsessed with the reconquest of Jerusalem.

Innocent's call for a new Crusade did not meet with the same enthusiasm that Urban II's call had. The nobles had seen how ruinously expensive earlier Crusades had been. To entice them, the pope devised a new way to finance the Crusade, a tax levied on all the clergy. The tax made it possible for a noble to earn a profit on the expedition. This potential for profit would entirely undermine the Fourth Crusade. Unlike the first three, which had been fought at least in part out of religious motives, the Fourth Crusade turned into a scramble for money and was the most corrupt of any of the campaigns to the Holy Land, which the Crusaders never even reached.

Enter the Venetians

In November 1199 the first Crusaders arrived in Champagne, France. From there, the leaders dispatched envoys (people sent on missions to represent the interests of someone else) to the great merchant city of Venice, Italy, to arrange transportation. Venice was ruled by the aging and blind, but still crafty, doge (or duke) Enrico Dandolo. For a hefty payment, Dandolo agreed to transport the Crusaders. He also agreed to provide fifty armed ships as escorts. In addition to a flat fee per person, based on an estimated number of men, the Crusaders were to pay to Venice half of everything they seized, whether land, money, or personal property. These terms were steep, but the envoys approved the arrangement and returned to France.

The Crusaders left France for Venice in June 1202. When they arrived, they were short on the price they had agreed to pay, primarily because not as many Crusaders were participating as had been anticipated. Early projections were that about thirty-three thousand men would join; in fact, only about eleven thousand arrived in Venice. Since the doge's price was based on the early estimate of the number of men, this meant that each of the Crusaders had to pay three times as much as he had expected to pay. The barons tried to make up the difference by selling off many of their personal goods, but they were still more than a third short.

The attack on Zara

To make up the difference, the doge offered a proposition. In the Adriatic Sea, not far from Venice, was an island town called Zara. Zara had long belonged to Venice but had recently pledged its allegiance to the king of Hungary. If the Crusaders would attack Zara and reclaim it for Venice, they could pay the money they still owed from any booty they seized in the city.

At first, the Crusaders were hesitant; Zara was a Christian city, and the king of Hungary supported the pope. Faced with little choice and running out of provisions, however, the Crusaders reluctantly agreed, and in November 1202 they attacked Zara. The inhabitants of the town hung banners with crosses over the city walls, trying to persuade the Crusaders to abandon their plan. Their efforts failed, however. The town offered little resistance and fell in just five days. The Crusaders plundered the city and divided half of the spoils.

Onward to Byzantium

On the day after Easter in 1203, the Crusaders, aboard Dandolo's ships, set sail to the east. Rather than heading toward Palestine, the fleet set a course for the coast of the Byzantine Empire and its capital city of Constantinople. Behind this change of plans was the doge. Just as the pope was obsessed with Jerusalem, the doge was obsessed with Constantinople and the trading profits that could be earned there.

Byzantium had been in decline since the death of the emperor Manuel in 1180. Ongoing warfare with the Seljuks had weakened the realm. One of Manuel's successors was a bumbling figure named Isaac Angelus, who was imprisoned by his brother, known as Emperor Alexius III. Alexius III annoyed the Dandolo, for he was giving more favorable trading terms to the merchants of Pisa and Genoa than to Venice.

Imprisoned with Angelus was his son, also named Alexius. In 1201 Prince Alexius escaped and fled to Venice, where he pleaded with the doge and the Crusaders to liberate

An early thirteenth-century Byzantine mosaic depicting the fall of Constantinople to the Crusaders on April 12, 1204. *The Art Archive/Dagli Ort. Reproduced by permission.*

Constantinople from Alexius III. In return, he offered the doge a large sum of money. To tempt the Crusaders, young Alexius promised that the Eastern Orthodox Church would pledge its allegiance to the pope.

The Crusaders, their heads filled with visions of the loot they could carry away from the city, sailed to the port city of Scutari, just on the outskirts of Constantinople. As they invaded the city, its defenders fled, along with Alexius III. The doge released Isaac Angelus from prison and decreed that Isaac and his son would rule jointly. On August 1, 1203, the son was crowned Alexius IV. But the empire was almost bankrupt. Popular resentment was rising over the large sums of money Alexius had pledged to the doge and to the Crusaders, which he now had to collect from his subjects. Both the clergy and the people resisted Alexius's call for submission to the Latin church (the Roman Catholic Church in the West).

Meanwhile, a fire broke out that burned for eight days and destroyed a large part of the city. The population was incensed (angry), but the object of their ire (hatred) was Alexius, for bringing the Venetian fleet to their city. The people rose up in revolt; one of Alexius's most trusted advisers seized the emperor in his sleep and had him strangled to death. A few days later Isaac died. To the satisfaction of the citizenry, the adviser proclaimed himself Emperor Alexius V.

The sack of Constantinople

The Crusaders, though, refused to recognize Alexius V as the new emperor, regarding him as a usurper (someone who had seized power by force and without any right to it) to the throne. So on April 8, 1204, the Crusaders attacked the city. The Byzantines held out for a few days, but on April 12 the Crusaders breached the walls, Alexius V fled, and the Crusaders rushed the city. The scene was utter chaos as drunken Crusaders rampaged through the city, taking everything they could get their hands on.

The Crusaders were overwhelmed by the richness of the booty that surrounded them. Although the empire itself was nearly bankrupt, the church and the people held enormous wealth, and the empire had gathered treasures from every part of the known world. At the Cathedral of Santa Sophia (often called the Hagia Sophia), the Crusaders took columns of silver from the choir stalls, as well as more golden chalices (drinking cups) and silver candelabra (branched candlesticks) than they could carry. Throughout the city, they seized vases, utensils, and other objects made of gold and silver as well as precious stones, furs, silks, and money. They looted holy relics, remnants of objects that were held sacred because of their association with saints, and ransacked the emperor's sumptuous five-hundred-room palace. Much of this loot was still on display in Venice in the early twenty-first century. Visitors to the Cathedral of San Marco could see there, over the cathedral's entrance, the most famous piece of booty the doge took: the Quadriga, four magnificent bronze horses that Emperor Constantine had brought back from Egypt nine centuries earlier.

On May 16, 1204, Count Baldwin of Flanders was crowned emperor in a lavish ceremony at the Cathedral of Santa Sophia. Thus began what historians call the Latin Empire of the East, but the new empire was not destined to last

The Cathedral of Santa
Sophia (often called the
Hagia Sophia) in
Constantinople. During the
Fourth Crusade the Christians
looted the cathedral, taking
everything of value back to
Europe with them. *©David
Samuel Robbins/Corbis.
Reproduced by permission.* 106

for long, just fifty-seven years. Baldwin's subjects were resentful of his efforts to impose Latin Christianity on the realm, and the empire soon began to crumble.

The Fourth Crusade thus came to an inglorious end. Nothing further was said about the infidel, the holy city, or the tomb of Christ. The Crusaders returned home, many of them laden with riches. A few remained in the empire and

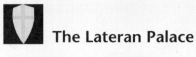

The Lateran Palace

At the time of Pope Innocent III, the Lateran Palace (rather than the modern-day Vatican) was the pope's residence and the seat of the church. It is part of a complex of courtyards, chapels, and halls and includes a magnificent basilica.

The Lateran buildings are built on Lateran Hill. During the reign of the Roman emperor Nero, a strange legend developed about the origin of the name Lateran. It said that the name came from the Latin expression *latitans rana,* which means "runaway frog." Nero was insane, so insane that he once decided that he wanted to be the mother of a baby, and he ordered his doctors to make him pregnant. The doctors, whose only alternative was being put to death, made the emperor swallow a tadpole, which, they claimed, would make him "pregnant" with a frog growing in his stomach. The doctors then pretended to "bring forth" the frog in birth by administering a purgative (a substance that induces vomiting). Nero was so proud of the frog that he formed an elaborate procession to show it off through the streets of Rome. But when the procession reached the banks of a nearby river, the frog jumped into the water and swam away. Angered, Nero killed the frog's nurse.

ruled over small parts of it. The aged doge had increased his wealth and the power of Venice immeasurably. The last portion of the thousand-plus-year-old Roman Empire was no more. And the Saracens (the Europeans' word for Middle Eastern Muslims) still controlled Jerusalem.

The Fifth Crusade

Nothing would change with the Fifth Crusade, which was fated to be yet another disaster for Christians in the East. Jerusalem had signed a treaty with al-Adil, the Syrian chief who controlled the city, and for fifteen years peace reigned in the region. With the treaty due to expire in 1215, the king of Jerusalem appealed to the pope for a new Crusade.

Pope Innocent III was happy to oblige. He wanted to keep the crusading spirit alive, because doing so would keep the people under the control of the church. He called for a church council at the Lateran Palace in Rome, the first such general council in the history of the church. There, with hundreds of the highest-ranking clerics in attendance, he established rules for a new Crusade. The Crusade was scheduled to depart for the Holy Land on June 1, 1217. Innocent, though, failed to see his dream realized, for he died in 1216.

In the spring of 1218 hundreds of ships from Germany and France arrived at Acre, where King John was already planning the Fifth Crusade. He had concluded that the best course of action was to attack Egypt, the richest country in the region. He had been urged to take this course by Italian traders and merchants, who hoped to accomplish in Egypt what the Fourth Crusade had accomplished in Constantinople. They convinced John that if the Saracens could be driven out of Egypt, the Crusaders would be able to attack Jerusalem from the south, while other troops would be able to attack from Acre. John was never a very firm leader, so he went along with this ill-advised plan. Once again, a Crusade would be fought for commercial interests rather than for religious purposes.

The siege of Damietta

The first goal was the port city of Damietta. Seize Damietta, and the Crusaders would have control of the Nile River and all of Egypt. The Crusader fleet departed for Damietta in May and sailed up the Nile in August 1218. When they arrived at Damietta, they found a heavily fortified city, so they laid a siege that lasted until November 1219, when the city finally fell.

The siege at Damietta turned into yet another error in the series of blunders the Christians committed. The pope sent a personal representative, a cardinal (the highest-ranking cleric, or member of the clergy, other than the pope) named Pelagius from Portugal. Pelagius was a ruthless, severe man who had no interest in negotiating with the Saracens. His single-minded goal was to fight them. He believed that as long as any were left, they would continue to be a threat. His stubbornness would doom the Fifth Crusade.

As it was becoming clear to the Egyptian sultan that he could not hold Damietta, much less all of Egypt, he offered peace terms to the Crusaders. His terms were nothing short of astounding. If the Crusaders would pack up and leave, he would turn over the relic of the True Cross, and his brother, the ruler of Syria, would give the Crusaders all of

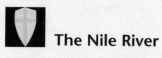

The Nile River

The Nile is the longest river in the world. Its principal source is Lake Victoria in east-central Africa. Flowing through Uganda, Sudan, and Egypt to the Mediterranean, it spans a distance of 3,470 miles (5,585 kilometers)—4,160 miles (6,695 kilometers) from its remotest headstream in Burundi. The river flows south to north, so traveling "up" the Nile means taking a southward route.

The Nile river basin covers an area of 1.1 million square miles (1.8 million square kilometers). While the Nile's waters in modern times are controlled by dams, at the time of the Crusades the entire basin would flood each year, leaving behind moist silt in which the next year's crops would be planted. It would be impossible to overestimate the economic importance of the Nile to the region and to Egypt, in particular. The only fertile lands in this otherwise desert country are found along the river basin, so it has always been a principal source of food and a major trade artery. The Egyptian pyramids and the Sphinx at Giza are located within view of the Nile.

Palestine, including Jerusalem. In return, all he asked was that trade routes between Egypt and Syria remain open.

The goal for which the Crusaders had been fighting for decades was within their grasp. All they had to do was to agree to al-Kamil's proposal and go home. But to the bewilderment of most of the Crusaders, Pelagius said no. In his refusal he was supported by the Italians, who had no use for Jerusalem. They wanted Damietta, one of the greatest port cities on the Mediterranean. A few days later, they got their wish when the city fell.

In the summer of 1221 John and Pelagius set out from Damietta toward Cairo with a force of five thousand knights and forty thousand foot soldiers. On July 24 they found themselves confronted by the sultan's army. The Nile River was rising, and the sultan ordered his men to destroy one of the dikes holding it back. The rushing waters trapped the Crusaders in a sea of mud. As they stumbled about trying to escape, the sultan's cavalry cut them down by the thousands. Pelagius found a boat and made it back to Damietta, where he pleaded for peace. The sultan agreed to an eight-year truce if the Crusaders would leave. On September 8,

1221, the remnants of the Fifth Crusade left Damietta. Once again, the West had suffered a humiliating defeat without getting anywhere near the city of Jerusalem.

The Sixth Crusade

The Sixth Crusade won back Jerusalem without shedding a single drop of blood. Behind this remarkable achievement was the Holy Roman Emperor, Frederick II, the grandson of Frederick Barbarossa. Frederick was the most powerful ruler in Europe at the time. He came to be known by the Latin expression *Stupor Mundi,* the "Wonder of the World." It was to him that Europe looked to finally win back Jerusalem.

Frederick had first taken the cross (made a vow to go to the Holy Land and free it) at his coronation in 1215, but for twelve years he did nothing. He wanted to lead a Crusade, but on his own terms and not out of submission to a pope. He had no interest in religious ideology (firmly held beliefs) or in defeating Islam. He wanted to extend his kingdom. For Frederick, adding Jerusalem to his realm would cement his place in history as the Wonder of the World.

Meanwhile, King John of Jerusalem was growing old. He knew that the throne would soon pass to his daughter, Isabella Yolanda. Like all the daughters of the Crusader kings, Isabella could inherit the crown but could not rule the Kingdom of Jerusalem herself. John had to find her a husband who would be suitable as king. The pope suggested a marriage between Isabella and Frederick, whose wife had recently died. Such a marriage, in a single stroke, would solve the succession problem, place a firm and skilled leader on the throne of Jerusalem, and likely persuade Frederick to honor his vow to lead a Crusade.

Everyone agreed with this plan, and in 1225 the wedding took place in Italy. Isabella, only fourteen at the time, was crowned queen, but the understanding was that her father would remain king until his death. Frederick, though, eager to seize power, backed out of the agreement and forced John to yield the crown to him. Frederick thus became king of Jerusalem without having set foot in the Holy Land.

Frederick's "reign" was short, for Isabella soon gave birth. Their son, Conrad, was now the king of Jerusalem, and Frederick could rule only as regent (a person who rules for a king or queen who is still a child). He knew the barons could elect someone else as regent whenever they wanted. He concluded that his only option was a show of overwhelming force that would bully the barons into submission. To that end, he first landed on the island of Cyprus, where he intimidated the nobles and even imprisoned the sons of the island's king. The king and his nobles, having little choice, agreed to support Frederick as regent for Conrad.

For years the emperor had been carrying on a correspondence with the sultan of Egypt, al-Malik al-Kamil. In these letters, many of them friendly exchanges about philosophy and literature, Frederick learned that al-Kamil had had a falling-out with the sultan of Damascus, his brother al-Mu'azzam Shams-al-Din Turan-Shah. Al-Mu'azzam was actually assembling an army to invade Egypt, and al-Kamil explored the possibility of forming an alliance with Frederick to prevent that from happening. Frederick's delay, though, almost lost him this potential ally, for al-Mu'azzam died, and al-Kamil did not see the new sultan of Damascus as a threat. By the time Frederick reached Acre, al-Kamil had lost interest in an alliance. But the new sultan of Damascus proved to be just as much of a threat to Egypt as al-Mu'azzam had been, so al-Kamil reopened negotiations with Frederick.

Al-Kamil, though, needed to save face with other Muslim leaders. Ever the skilled diplomat, Frederick agreed to help al-Kamil stage an elaborate charade. Frederick marched his army of three thousand knights in one direction, al-Kamil marched toward them, and when the two armies met, the two commanders sat down to "negotiate," though they had already agreed on terms.

On February 18, 1229, the two met in Jaffa and signed a treaty. Under the terms of the Treaty of Jaffa, al-Kamil agreed to hand over Jerusalem, Bethlehem, and Nazareth, as well as a strip of land that would give Jerusalem access to the sea. In return, Muslims would be allowed free access to Jerusalem, and Muslim holy places in the city would remain in Muslim hands. With the stroke of a pen, Jerusalem was finally restored to Christians. It was one of the few occasions when diplomacy (negotiations) would replace the sword.

The treaty was condemned by all sides. Muslims throughout the region were angered that al-Kamil had given up Jerusalem without a fight. Some of the more bloodthirsty Crusaders were angry because they were denied the opportunity to kill Saracens. Frederick, however, brushed aside these objections. He was determined to be crowned king of Jerusalem, but when he entered the city on March 17, 1229, everyone ignored him. The next day, Frederick went to the Church of the

Holy Sepulchre and declared himself king. The only people who witnessed the ceremony were his own troops.

Frederick returned to Acre, where he found that many of the barons were conspiring against him. Then word reached him that the pope had assembled an army to invade Frederick's territory in the south of Italy. Frederick knew that he had to go to defend his realm. After replacing the Franks who had ruled in the Crusader states for so long with as many Germans as he could, he departed from Acre on May 1, 1229. Scorned by most of Acre's population, he tried to sneak out early in the morning. As he passed through a section of the town called the Butcher's Quarter, the butchers recognized him and ran after him, pelting him with fish guts.

The Seventh Crusade

The Treaty of Jaffa called for ten years of peace, but the Franks spent those ten years in a state of near civil war, further weakening their hold on Outremer. Then, in 1244, another clan of Muslim Turks, the Khwarismians, attacked Jerusalem, leaving few Christian survivors. The desperate Franks tried to form an alliance with the Syrian Muslims to drive the Turks out, but the Turks, in concert with the Egyptians, decisively defeated them in the Battle of Harbiyah in October of that year.

The response in Europe was the Seventh Crusade, which was led by the extremely devout (religious) King Louis IX of France. Louis left Europe in the summer of 1248 and arrived in the Holy Land with his army in 1249. He easily recaptured Damietta in June. Then he marched south on the city of Mansurah. He laid siege to the city, but on February 8, 1250, the Egyptian forces attacked, cutting off the Crusaders' supply routes. Louis held out until April, but his troops were starving, and Louis himself was ill. The Crusaders tried to retreat, but the Egyptians pursued them until Louis was forced to surrender. Louis and his knights were taken captive, but eventually they were ransomed and returned to Europe. Louis ransomed himself by returning Damietta.

Once again, a Crusade to save the Holy Land had failed, and the Crusaders never came near their goal. Europe was growing sick of crusading, few western Christians remained in the region, and all that remained was for those last few to be driven out.

For More Information

Books

Billings, Malcolm. *The Crusades: Five Centuries of Holy Wars*. New York: Sterling, 1996.

Fulcher of Chartres. *A History of the Expedition to Jerusalem, 1095–1127*. Translated by Frances Rita Ryan. Knoxville: University of Tennessee Press, 1969.

Hamilton, Franklin. *The Crusades*. New York: Dial Press, 1965.

Jones, Terry, and Alan Ereira. *Crusades*. New York: Facts on File, 1995.

Riley-Smith, Jonathan. *The Crusades: A Short History*. New Haven, CT: Yale University Press, 1987.

Runciman, Steven. *A History of the Crusades*. 3 vols. Cambridge, U.K.: Cambridge University Press, 1951–1954.

Web Sites

Madden, Thomas F. "The Real History of the Crusades." *Catholic Educator's Resource Center.* http://www.catholiceducation.org/articles/history/world/wh0055.html (accessed on August 11, 2004).

Muslim Response to the Crusades and the Cairo/ Baghdad Caliphate Split

In the late 1090s the European Crusaders in Syria and Palestine were fighting on foreign soil and in harsh, desert conditions to which they were not accustomed. They were far from their homelands and sources of supply. Further, their numbers were not very large; perhaps twenty thousand Crusaders made it to Jerusalem. After the city fell to the Crusaders in 1099, only a few thousand remained in Jerusalem and the other Crusader states, including Antioch, Edessa, and Tripoli. Jerusalem remained defended by only about three hundred knights. Muslims, meanwhile, had shown themselves to be skilled warriors for centuries, as their empire grew throughout the region, across North Africa, and into Spain. Yet the Crusaders did not face a serious threat for more than four decades.

Historians give two related answers to explain why. One is that many Muslims did not regard the Crusaders as a serious threat to them, at least initially. The other is that Islam, the religion practiced by Muslims, was too divided for Muslims to mount a serious response to the Crusades. Because of these divisions, each faction, or subgroup, within Islam tended to see the other factions as greater threats than the Crusaders. Thus, to understand fully the Muslim response, or lack of response, to the Crusaders, it is necessary to understand these divisions within Islam.

The major participants

At the time of the First Crusade (1095–99) and in the years that followed, a number of major "players" occupied the Middle East.

- Sunni Muslims: The Sunnis were the largest sect, or subgroup, of Muslims. These were the orthodox, or mainstream, Muslims who believed that the rightful successors to Muhammad, the founder of Islam, were the caliphs (Islamic spiritual leaders).

- Abbasids: Abbasid was the name of the ruling dynasty of Sunni Muslims. They claimed to be descendants of Muhammad's uncle, Abbas. The Abbasid caliphate (the office of the caliph as well as his domain) ruled the Muslim empire from the capital city of Baghdad in Persia (modern-day Iraq).

- Seljuks: The Seljuks were Turks who had converted to Sunni Islam. The Seljuk Empire was ruled by a Turkish sultan (the ruler of a Muslim state) from the city of Isfahan, in western Iran. While the Abbasids were the spiritual leaders of Sunni Muslims, the Seljuks held the real political power because they had the military might.

- Shiites: The Shiites were a dissident, or rebel, faction of Islam. Their name came from the phrase *Shi'at Ali,* meaning "party of Ali." They believed that Muhammad's blood relative Ali should have been named caliph after Muhammad's death. To the Shiites, the Sunni Abbasids and the dynasty that preceded them, the Umayyads, were corrupt, or false. They fought the Sunnis for control of the Islamic faith (see Chapter 5 on the division between the Sunnis and the Shiites).

- Fatimids: The Fatimids were a Shiite dynasty that ruled Egypt. They believed they were the descendants of Muhammad's daughter Fatima. They ruled from an independent caliphate in the capital city of Cairo. The Fatimids had been in control of Jerusalem until 1071, when the Seljuks drove them out, though they retook the city in 1098.

Response to the First Crusade

As the Crusaders made their way down the eastern coast of the Mediterranean Sea to Jerusalem, they occupied a number of cities, including Antioch and Edessa. To escape the Crusaders, many Muslim refugees from these cities fled farther inland to such cities as Damascus and Aleppo, both in Syria. There they began to demand a response to the Crusaders. One

An illustration depicting the battle between the Muslims and the Crusaders for Jerusalem in 1099.
©Bettmann/Corbis.
Reproduced by permission.

A slip-painted pottery bowl, with an archer on horseback. The bowl was probably created by a Muslim refugee who fled to Aleppo to escape the Christian Crusaders.
Copyright The British Museum. Reproduced by permission.

leader who listened to their pleas was al-Harawi, who was the chief *qadi* (a position similar to mayor) of Damascus. Al-Harawi traveled to Baghdad to persuade the Abbasid caliph, al-Mustazhir Billah, to send troops to confront the Crusaders.

Al-Harawi encountered two problems, though. One was that Baghdad was a long distance from Jerusalem, so the caliph did not see the Crusaders as a serious threat. The other was that the caliph had no army to send. Military power resided with the Seljuk Turks and their sultan, Barkiyaruq, in the Iranian city of Isfahan. Isfahan, however, was even farther away from Jerusalem than was Baghdad, so the sultan was even less concerned about the Crusader threat.

Moreover, the Turkish sultan had problems of his own. He was young and inexperienced, and after the death of his father in 1094 he had to fight off rivals for the sultanate and even members of his own military. Syria and Palestine, to him, were distant outposts, so he showed little interest in helping. He was more interested in the closer cities of Damascus, Aleppo, and Mosul. These cities were part of the Seljuk Empire, but they were ruled by Seljuk officers who were more concerned with maintaining their own power than in submitting to the sultan.

During the tenth century Muslims had fought against the Byzantine Christians and won some major battles in the 950s. But by the end of the eleventh century, waging war against Christians was not a priority. The Turks and the Abassids tended to see the Crusaders as nothing more than soldiers for hire of the Byzantine Christians, who had already been defeated and whose empire was shrinking.

Ironically, that is just what the Crusaders were supposed to have been. The First Crusade was called in response to pleas from the Byzantine emperor. The emperor of Byzantium, the seat of the Eastern Orthodox Christian religion, believed that he could drive the Seljuks out of Byzantine territory if he expanded his army with knights from Europe. He knew, though, that Europeans probably would not help him if he appealed to them to restore his empire. He appealed to them instead on religious grounds (see "A Cry for Help" in Chapter 4). His plan backfired, however. While Crusaders came and fought the Seljuks, they were not fighting for the Byzantine emperor. They and the pope of the Catholic Church in Rome had their own religious goals, and many of the Crusaders were driven by a strong desire to win territory of their own.

The Sunni Muslims, though, did not recognize this threat. Their main concern remained trying to find a way to put down the Shiites, who, from the Sunni perspective, were a greater threat than the Crusaders. Most, though not all,

A Seljuk relief sculpture of warriors. To the Seljuks, the Crusaders were more of a distraction from their fight against the Shiites, especially the Fatimids. ©*Archivo Iconografico, S.A./Corbis. Reproduced by permission.*

Shiites believed the claims made by the separate caliphate in Cairo, Egypt: that the Fatimids were the legitimate successors to Muhammad because they were descended from Muhammad's daughter. The chief focus of the Egyptians was fighting the Sunni Seljuks for control of Palestine and Syria. Regarding the Seljuks as their real enemy, they often formed alliances with the Christians, for they saw the Christians, at least initially, as the only allies they had in fighting the

Seljuks. The key point is that at the time of the First Crusade, two independent caliphates—a Sunni caliphate based in Baghdad and a Shiite caliphate based in Cairo—were more worried about each other than they were about an unruly mob of western Christians in their lands. To the Seljuks, the Crusaders were merely a distraction from their fight against the Shiites, especially the Fatimids.

One way to measure the level of interest Muslims took in the Crusaders is to examine mentions of the Crusaders in the literature of the time. A few Arab poets condemned the Crusaders, and several decades after the First Crusade, several of them celebrated such events as the recapture of Edessa in 1144 (see "The Second Crusade" in Chapter 6). Other poets, though, wrote about their relationships with the Crusaders in more tolerant ways. Some expressed great admiration for the beauty of European women. Others wrote of friendships that they had formed with the Crusaders. Some voiced admiration for the bravery of the Crusaders and their willingness to die, though they were quite troubled by how dirty the Europeans were. They were also puzzled by the European custom of shaving their faces, for Islamic teaching dictated that men should wear beards. Still other poets ignored the presence of the Crusaders. Arab historians at the time noted the presence of the Crusaders but little else. Much of their surviving work is about the quarrels between Sunnis and Shiites rather than about the Crusaders. Had the Crusaders been seen as a serious threat, rather than a nuisance, it is likely that the Arab literature of the time would have expressed more outrage and called to expel them (drive them out).

The counter-Crusade begins

Only slowly did the Muslims of Syria and Palestine begin to recognize the religious aims of the Crusaders, who did not appear to be going home. They began to search for a leader who could drive out the Crusaders, but they knew that they could not count on Baghdad for help. The leader had to come from within Syria itself, possibly from Aleppo or Damascus.

The first effort to fight back was launched by the *qadi* of Aleppo, who recruited a Turkish emir (commander), Ilghazi, from a nearby town to lead the fight against the Crusaders. In 1119 his army, together with an army led by the emir of Damascus, marched on the city of Antioch, and on June 28 they defeated a Crusader army led by the Christian ruler of Antioch, Roger. This was a major blow to the Crusaders, but little came of it. Ilghazi, an alcoholic, died just three years later without having followed up on his victory.

In the 1120s another leader emerged, Ilghazi's nephew Balak. Balak inspired a great deal of fear in the Crusaders. One western historian of the time, Fulcher of Chartres, referred to him as "the Raging Dragon." In 1122 he captured Joscelin, the cousin of the king of Jerusalem, Baldwin II. Then in 1123 he captured the king himself. By 1124 Balak was the ruler of Aleppo, and he began to reconquer territory held by the Christians. But fate intervened. In 1124 the Muslims of Tyre (in present-day Lebanon) called on Balak to rescue them from a Crusader siege of the city. Just before he departed, he was inspecting his troops and the fortifications, or defenses, around Aleppo when a stray arrow struck him in the chest and he died. Once again, Syrian Muslims were left without a leader. In the meantime, the Assassins, a secretive Shiite sect (see "The Assassins" in Chapter 5), continued to try to overthrow the Sunnis. They assassinated the emirs of Aleppo and Mosul, further undermining any united Muslim response to the Crusaders.

Zengi, Nur al-Din, and Saladin

Serious *jihad,* or holy war, against the Crusaders came from another Seljuk Turk, Imad al-Din Zengi. In 1126 Zengi rose to power in Baghdad. There, the Abbasid caliph tried to free the caliphate from the Seljuks and led an uprising. Zengi was the Turkish general who put down the uprising. In the 1130s he began to reconquer lands in Syria. This effort came to a climax in 1144, when he laid siege to the city of Edessa and finally entered the city on Christmas Eve of that year.

After Zengi's death in 1146, his son, Nur al-Din, remained in charge of Aleppo. The emir of Damascus, though, did not trust al-Din, whom he saw as an ambitious Turk with the aim of conquering all of Syria. Nevertheless, he tried to keep peace with al-Din. At this point, the European Chris-

pud me oracio deo urte mee: di
cam deo susceptor meus es.

tians made a major blunder. They could have kept Aleppo and Damascus divided, but the fall of Edessa to Zengi prompted calls for the Second Crusade in Europe (see "The Second Crusade" in Chapter 6). When the Crusaders, led by French king Louis VII, arrived in the Holy Land in 1149, they attacked Damascus, the Crusaders' only ally in the region. With little choice, the emir of Damascus called on al-Din to come to the defense of the city. The Second Crusade ended in a humiliating defeat for the Crusaders and succeeded only in strengthening al-Din. In 1154 Damascus fell to al-Din's forces.

The conflict between Sunnis and Shiites, however, continued. Al-Din, rather than focusing his attention on the Crusaders, turned instead against Egypt and the Shiite Fatimid dynasty. To fight him off, the Egyptians formed an alliance with the Crusaders, but while fighting was going on in Egypt, al-Din successfully attacked near Antioch and captured a large number of Crusader troops, as well as their leaders.

Muslim leader Saladin in combat with Richard I, king of England. It was only after Saladin patched together a shaky alliance between Muslim leaders in the Middle East that he was able to confront the Crusaders led by Richard.

Finally, in 1169, al-Din's forces defeated the Fatimids and entered Cairo. At their head was al-Din's nephew, Saladin. Saladin would go on to play a major role in the Third Crusade, but in the meantime he spent the next decade or so subduing other Muslim leaders in the region. Only after he patched together a shaky alliance, or union, with them was he able to confront the Crusader forces led by King Richard I of England.

In sum, it took decades for the Muslims to understand that the Crusaders planned to be a permanent presence in the region. Only then, in the mid-twelfth century, were they able to begin to recapture some of their territory. The capture of Edessa was a turning point, for it represented the first loss of a major Crusader city. From then on, the rest of the history of the Crusades was largely one of defeat, or at best stalemate, for the Crusaders. Still, because of divisions in Islam, it took nearly a century for Muslims to respond effectively to the Crusaders.

For More Information

Books

Gabrieli, Francesco. *Arab Historians of the Crusades*. Translated by E. J. Costello. Berkeley: University of California Press, 1969.

Riley-Smith, Jonathan, ed. *The Oxford Illustrated History of the Crusades*. New York: Oxford University Press, 1995.

Runciman, Steven. *A History of the Crusades*. 3 vols. Cambridge, U.K.: Cambridge University Press, 1951–1954.

Periodicals

Irwin, Robert. "Muslim Responses to the Crusades." *History Today*, 47, no. 4 (April 1997): 43–49.

Web Sites

Irwin, Robert. *History Today: Muslim Responses to the Crusades*. http://www.findarticles.com/p/articles/mi_m1373/is_n4_v47/ai_19 308695 (accessed on August 11, 2004).

Jewish People Caught in the Crusades

The darkest chapter in the history of the Crusades was the treatment of Jews at the hands of Europe's Christians, both in Europe and in the Middle East. What began as distrust and scorn often turned into widespread persecution and slaughter. Many Crusaders left in their wake the bodies of hundreds of Jews as they made their way to the Holy Land. Jews lost their homes, families, property, and lives in a frenzy of anti-Jewish feeling among many European Christians.

For centuries, Jewish people commemorated the horrors they endured during the Crusades. These memories were only partly overshadowed by the Holocaust of the twentieth century, the systematic extermination of Jews by the Nazi regime in Germany before and during World War II (1939–45). Referring to this later period of violence, the historian Malcolm Billings noted in his book *The Crusades: Five Centuries of Holy Wars,* "The road to the Holy Land ran through what Jews later came to describe as the first Holocaust."

The Jews of Europe

By the time Pope Urban II called the First Crusade in 1095 (see "The Sermon at Clermont" in Chapter 6), Jews had matured and established communities throughout Europe. In nearly every city of any size could be found synagogues (places of worship for Jews), schools, Jewish cemeteries, and rabbis (leaders of Jewish congregations), some of whom, because of their high level of education, consulted with and influenced civil rulers. These communities had their own local histories. Their religious identity, based on centuries-old rituals and use of the Hebrew language to record, pass down, and practice their traditions, set them apart from the surrounding Christian communities.

Many Christians came to see these Jewish communities as hostile to Christianity. Jews, in their view, were not part of "us," that is, of the Christian, feudal way of life. They were "others," a people apart from that way of life, and in that respect they were no different from Muslims. They looked different, dressed differently, spoke a different language, practiced their religion in a different manner, and for the most part did not assimilate into (become absorbed into) the surrounding French, German, English, Spanish, or other communities.

More and more throughout the tenth and eleventh centuries, European Christians feared the threat from the Muslim empire, the empire that had formed around the Islamic faith and the teachings of the founder of Islam, Muhammad. This empire had expanded throughout the Mediterranean region and into Spain (see "The Spread of Islam" in Chapter 1) and in the eighth century had to be driven back out of France. Faced with this fear, Christians were accustomed to referring to "enemies of God" and calling for vengeance, or revenge, on those enemies. While Jews posed no such threat, they were not Christians, so they too fell under the heading of "enemies."

Also during this period, there developed among Christians a "cult of the cross." The cross referred to was the one on which Christ was nailed when he was put to death. Crusaders, when they vowed to go to the Holy Land (Jerusalem and the surrounding region) to free it, were said to have "taken the cross." As a symbol of their promise, they wore a cross on their armor and shields. During the reign of the Roman emperor Constantine in the fourth cen-

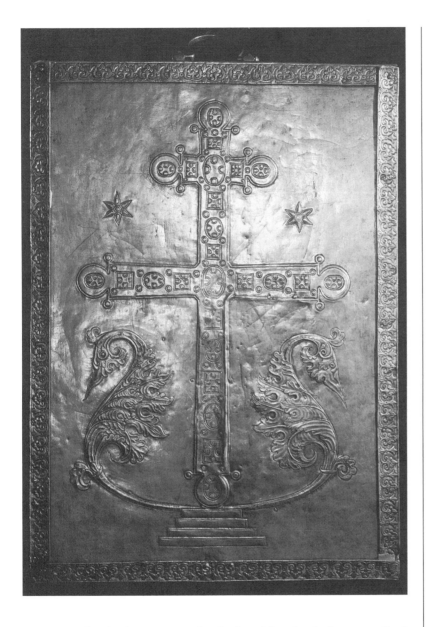

This reliquary contains the True Cross, the actual cross on which Jesus Christ died. When Crusaders vowed to go to the Holy Land, they were said to have "taken the cross." *©Werner Forman/ Corbis. Reproduced by permission.*

tury, a relic (a fragment of a holy object) of the so-called True Cross, the actual cross on which Christ died, was found in Jerusalem. In the centuries that followed, the image of a suffering Christ hanging on the cross, the Catholic crucifix, became central to the faith. Veneration of (devotion to) the crucifix, in turn, led to a focus on Christ's death, and many Christians began to hold the Jews responsible for that death.

One way many Christians acted on this belief was to call for the conversion of the Jews to Christianity. But this belief began to take on more unreasonable forms. Many Christians came to believe, for example, that the Jews were somehow the "agents" of the Muslims in the Holy Land. In France charges were made that French Jews had urged Caliph Hakim to destroy the Church of the Holy Sepulchre, the site of the tomb of Christ, in Jerusalem in the early years of the eleventh century (see "Destruction of the Church of the Holy Sepulchre" in Chapter 2). These charges set off a wave of persecution against the Jews.

Other Christians convinced themselves that the Jews actively supported the Muslim occupation of the holy city of Jerusalem. This was at best a partial truth. Life for Jews was actually better under the Muslims after they took control of the city in 638 than it had been under the Byzantine Christians before that (see "Muslims and Jerusalem" in Chapter 2). None of this mattered, though. Jews, as non-Christians, were infidels, or nonbelievers. So were Muslims. Therefore, when Pope Urban II called the First Crusade, many European Christians interpreted his call to fight "infidelity," or lack of belief in the Christian faith, as a call to fight any infidel, that is, anyone who did not believe in Christianity. The nearest targets were Europe's Jews.

Massacres of European Jews

Persecution of the Jews lasted throughout the Crusades. For example, during the Second Crusade (1047–49) there were uprisings against Jews in the German city of Würzburg. Ronald C. Finucane, in *Soldiers of the Faith: Crusaders and Moslems at War,* quotes the powerful and important abbot (religious leader) of the monastery at Cluny, France, who wrote: "What is the good of going to the end of the world at great loss of men and money to fight the Saracens [Muslims], when we permit among us other infidels who are a thousand times more guilty towards Christ than the Mohammedans." At the time that one of the leaders of the Third Crusade (1189–92), Richard I, was being crowned king of England, anti-Jewish riots were breaking out in the city of York.

Much of the worst violence, though, took place during the First Crusade (1095–99; see "The First Crusade" in

An illustration of a massacre of the Jews during the Crusades. The Jews were targets because they did not believe in the Christian faith. ©*Leonard de Selva/ Corbis. Reproduced by permission.*

Chapter 6). Historians have many eyewitness accounts, both from Jews and non-Jews, of violence in cities such as Speyer, Mainz, Cologne, and Worms in the German Rhineland (that is, the area along the Rhine River), as well as in such cities as Regensburg (near Munich, Germany) and Prague (in the modern-day Czech Republic). These cities lay along the route that many Crusaders, particularly German Crusaders, followed to the Middle East.

Was Christopher Columbus Jewish?

Some people have theorized that Christopher Columbus, who sailed to the New World in 1492, the same year that the Jews were expelled from Spain, was himself Jewish, or at least that his voyage was financed by Jews. These Jews, according to the theory, were looking for a place of refuge and hoped that Columbus might find one across the Atlantic Ocean. There is little evidence to support this theory other than the fact that the crew member who served as a translator for Columbus is known to have been well-versed in Hebrew. (For more on Columbus and his connection with the Crusades, see "The Jews Are Expelled from Spain" in Chapter 13.)

One city whose Jews were hard hit was Worms. Jews in the city heard that those in Speyer were being attacked, so they asked the Christian bishop of Worms for protection. Many even gave him their savings for safekeeping. But as the Crusaders descended on the city in May 1096, they began murdering Jewish men, women, and children. Led by a German named Emicho from the city of Leiningen, they plundered (robbed) the homes of Jews, seizing whatever wealth they could find. Many Crusaders used stolen Jewish wealth to finance their journey to the Holy Land. They destroyed the Jewish cemetery just outside the walls of the city. They looted the city's magnificent Byzantine-style synagogue. They tried to force Jews to be baptized as Christians. Those who refused were either killed or committed suicide. In many instances, Jewish men killed their wives and children rather than allow them to be brutalized by the Crusaders. In all, about eight hundred people died.

The Crusaders then moved on to Mainz, where similar scenes were replayed during the summer of 1096. Again, Jews in Mainz heard about events in Worms, so they appealed to the Christian archbishop for protection. Once more they tried to buy protection—this time, from the local count—with silver and gold. But it was no use. The Crusaders again stormed the city. Some Jews, trapped in the archbishop's palace and grounds, where he tried to protect them, attempted to fight back, but they stood no chance. Others taunted the Christians, hurling insults about Christ and his mother, Mary. These insults, of course, only inflamed the Crusaders. In Mainz, too, many men, seeing that they had no hope of surviving the onslaught, committed suicide, first sacrificing their families. About nine hundred Jews were killed in the city.

An illustrated page from William of Tyre's book *A History of Deeds Done beyond the Sea.* *Reproduced by permission of The British Library (Yates Thompson 12).*

Efforts to help

Not all European Christians shared in this blood lust against the Jews. Many members of the Christian clergy tried to excommunicate, or expel from the church, those who were persecuting the Jews. Numerous local nobles threatened Crusaders with punishment, but they had no way to back up the threat. One historian of the time, William of Tyre, an archbishop, wrote in *A History of Deeds Done beyond the Sea* of the "mad excesses" of the Crusaders, who "cruelly massacred the Jewish people in the cities and towns through which they passed."

During the Second Crusade, the preaching of Bernard, the abbot at the monastery at Clairvaux in France, like that of Pope Urban II at the start of the First Crusade, aroused enthusiasm for the undertaking (see "The Second Crusade" in Chapter 6 and "Knights Templars" in Chapter 9). Bernard sought to use his great influence to stop the bloodshed. He tried, for example, to silence a monk in the

A print depicting the conquest of Jerusalem during the First Crusade. Leaders of the Crusade are Peter the Hermit (left) and Louis VI (right), while the image in the center shows Crusaders massacring Jewish residents of the city. *©Leonard de Selva/Corbis. Reproduced by permission.*

Rhineland who was calling on the Crusaders to attack Jews and whipping up anti-Jewish feelings. When he wrote to England, urging the nation to join the Crusade, he cautioned the English against persecution of the Jews.

Many other people tried to help. One historian in Würzburg recorded the story of a Christian washerwoman who found a young Jewish girl inside a Christian church. The girl had been beaten, spat upon, and left for dead. The woman took the girl home, tended her wounds, and gave her shelter. The bishop of the city, pained by the actions of the Crusaders, ordered that the bodies of Jews be collected, cleaned, and anointed with oil in preparation for burial. The bodies were then buried in the bishop's own garden.

The massacres at Worms, Mainz, and other cities did not satisfy the Crusaders' thirst for Jewish blood, however. When the Crusaders stormed Jerusalem in 1099 (see "The First Crusade" in Chapter 6), they slaughtered not only Muslims but also most of the city's Jewish residents, who had taken refuge in the synagogue. This type of anti-Semitism, or hatred of Jews, persisted throughout the Crusades and beyond, as many Christians in Europe continued to see Jews as untrustworthy, as "Christ killers," and as strangers and foreigners.

European Jews in the centuries that followed the Crusades were systematically excluded from government jobs, the professions, and places of education. At various times, they suffered forced migrations if they refused to convert to Christianity: from England in 1290, France in 1394, and Spain in 1492. Because they were denied many "respectable" ways to earn a living, they often became moneylenders. In this way, they acquired an unfair reputation for greed. Especially inclined to this view were needy members of the middle and upper classes, who often turned to the Jews when they had to borrow money, scorning them even while taking it. One legacy of the Crusades was nearly a millennium of hostility and distrust between Christians and Jews, a legacy whose effects are still felt today.

For More Information

Books

Billings, Malcolm. *The Crusades: Five Centuries of Holy Wars*. New York: Sterling, 1996.

Chazan, Robert. *European Jewry and the First Crusade*. Berkeley: University of California Press, 1987.

Finucane, Ronald C. *Soldiers of the Faith: Crusaders and Moslems at War*. London: J. M. Dent, 1983.

Krey, August C. *The First Crusade: The Accounts of Eye-Witnesses and Participants*. Princeton, NJ: Princeton University Press, 1921.

William of Tyre. *A History of Deeds Done beyond the Sea*. 2 vols. Translated by Emily Atwater Babcock and A. C. Krey. New York: Columbia University Press, 1943.

Knights and the Traditions of Chivalry

9

Numerous foot soldiers gave their lives to the cause of reclaiming the Holy Land during the Crusades. Carrying the banners of that cause, though, was Europe's warrior class: its knights. Noble, courageous, and skilled, the knights of Europe, from the viewpoint of the Christian nations, carried out God's work in trying to drive the Muslims (followers of the religion of Islam) out of God's holy places. In the twenty-first century the image of these knights is often romanticized. The "knight in shining armor" occupies an honored, permanent place in the cultural heritage of the West and is a fixture in legends, fairy tales, and epic adventure stories (see Chapter 11 on the literature of the Crusades).

While knights are usually thought of in connection with medieval life, the tradition of conferring knighthood has not died, at least in England. In 1997 rock star Paul McCartney, one of the original Beatles of the 1960s, was knighted by England's Queen Elizabeth II during a ceremony in London. Another rock legend, Mick Jagger of the Rolling Stones, received a similar honor in 2004. Like their forebears hundreds of years ago, these modern knights, in a solemn and formal ceremony, knelt before the queen. The queen then tapped them on each shoulder with the flat side of a bared sword as she "invested" them with (gave them) the title "knight." From that time on, as a member of the nobility, each knight became entitled to attach the word "sir" to his name, though it is unlikely that either of these rock-and-roll icons will actually do so.

It is equally unlikely that Sir Paul, Sir Mick, or any of the other prominent artists and citizens of Great Britain who have been knighted in modern times will put on a suit of armor, mount a horse, and set out to conquer new realms for his queen. Knighthood for these and other citizens is granted to recognize cultural achievement or service to Great Britain, typically for charitable work. But the underlying concept of service to the realm has defined knighthood since the Middle Ages.

Closely connected with knighthood is the concept of chivalry. Today, people are likely to use the word *chivalry* to refer to high standards of good manners, protectiveness, and helpfulness. Most often the word crops up in relationships between men and women. A man who politely holds open a door for a woman or who defends her from danger is still said to be acting "chivalrously." The word reflects, as it did hundreds of years ago, a code of behavior that places value on the protection of others.

"Knighthood" and "chivalry" are not one and the same, but it is impossible to speak of one without addressing the other. And it is impossible to understand either without first looking at the social structure of medieval Europe. It was this social structure that gave rise to the institution of knighthood, including special orders of knighthood such as the Knights Hospitallers and Knights Templars. In turn, knighthood gave rise to the institution and codes of chivalry.

Origins

First we must consider the origins of the words. Despite the romantic, adventurous images that surround the words "knighthood" and "chivalry," the origins of the two words are rather homely. "Knight" is an Anglo-Saxon (Germanic-English) word. It comes from the Old English word *cniht,* which means simply "boy." It evolved into the word "knight" because many early knights were still in their teens when they began to serve as men-at-arms for their lords.

The word "chivalry," on the other hand, originates in the Romance languages (Italian, Spanish, and French). It comes from the Old French word *chevalerie,* which means something like "skill in handling a horse." In an age before guns, gunpowder, and cannons, warfare with lances and swords required the knight to battle his opponent personally and up close. Only those who could control and direct the strength and speed of a horse were likely to survive armed combat, although peasants and commoners, in contrast to members of the nobility, had to take their chances on foot. In many early texts, "chivalry" refers simply to the actual ranks of a mounted army, that is, to "troops." In time, though, the word came to stand for much more, in particular, a code of behavior and ethics to which all knights were expected to hold.

The structure of medieval society

To understand the institutions of knighthood and chivalry, and the motivations of many of the Crusaders (what drove them in their cause), it is necessary to examine the structure of life during the Middle Ages in Europe. This was the period of time roughly from 500 to 1500, also called the medieval period. Several characteristics of medieval life are important.

Land

First, land was the source of nearly all wealth. The Middle Ages began to see the appearance of a small middle class that earned its income through such activities as trade and finance. But most wealth during this time was the product of the land. Land provided lumber and stone to build houses, fuel, food crops, animal fur and fabrics for clothing—nearly all of the necessities of life. Those who owned large estates of land, in later years called "fiefs," had almost always received them as grants from a king for their service, usually in war. With the land came a noble title, such as duke, earl, or baron.

The king ruled absolutely—that is, with complete authority—over his subjects, just as God ruled absolutely over kings. Noble landowners, in turn, ruled absolutely over their smaller fiefdoms in a social and military system called feudalism. Feudalism began primarily in France, but in time it spread through much of Europe, including England. It emerged in the centuries following the withdrawal of the Romans, when Europe was overrun by marauding (raiding and looting), warlike tribes, many of them sweeping across from western Asia or south from Scandinavia. Without the order that the Roman Empire had imposed, life in much of Europe became a free-for-all. Armed bandits, warlords (military commanders), and bands of outlaws were commonplace. The general population had little protection from them. Feudalism provided some measure of security during an extremely insecure period of history.

To drive off these outlaws, the nobles needed to develop small armies of warriors who could pursue them and engage them in combat. The only way they could do so effectively was on horseback; foot soldiers simply could not keep up with the constant movement of plundering armies. Horses, though, were expensive, and it took years to train both the horse and the warrior who rode it. A man who hoped to become a mounted warrior could not do it on his own, because he lacked the time and means to support himself.

To support their cavalry soldiers, called vassals, nobles made grants of land to them. The vassal, in return, owed a duty of loyalty to his "liege lord." In times of peace he farmed and otherwise managed the land with the help of a large peasant class, but when that land came under threat, he owed service as a warrior. In turn, the lord had to provide his vassals with protection and the means of economic survival. This was the essence of feudalism: It was a system of shared legal obligations that bound together the lord and his vassals, as well as the peasantry beneath them. Its chief feature was a rigid hierarchy, or chain of command, with the king at the top, beneath him his barons, then vassals, then a lower order of knights, and, finally, the peasantry. Each level of the hierarchy owed military service to the level above.

In the early years of this system, during the eighth and ninth centuries, the vassal's grant of land was returned to the

Nobility

Texts about the European nobility present a potentially confusing array (collection) of titles, including ranks such as baron, earl, marquess (MAR-kwis), and count. Some of these titles were exclusive to the European continent, while others were distinctive of England. Still others were used both in England and on the Continent, but sometimes the ranks they indicated were different.

One source of confusion is that the titles did not always correspond to rule over a particular expanse of territory. Many were originally granted by a king for service and were simply hereditary ranks (those passed on from father to son). Holding the rank would entitle the nobleman to certain privileges, especially the right to collect income from his subjects and obtain a pension, or allowance, for his widow. A further source of confusion is that the same nobleman could have more than one title. Thus, for example, a duke could hold a secondary title as a marquess (or marquis). Similarly, that duke's son could hold a title as a lower-ranking noble.

One of the most common titles that appears in connection with the Crusades is baron. In Europe, a baron was among the highest-ranking members of the nobility. The title is a feudal one and was granted by the king to a tenant who held the position by virtue of military or other honorable service. Thus, it was not necessarily hereditary. The barons frequently functioned as the king's advisers, though they often competed with him

noble when the vassal died. By about the year 1000, though, this practice was changing, and the land would pass to the vassal's heir, generally his oldest son. The heir would then assume his father's place in the hierarchy. The fundamental duties of the vassal did not change. While he sat in council to give advice to his lord, heard local court cases as a judge or magistrate (an official in charge of the administration of laws), or guarded garrisons (military posts), his primary role was to fight. In this way the European vassals developed into a warrior class, much like the samurai became the warrior class of Japan. Many vassals themselves employed knights, enabling them to muster, or gather, a small army when the need arose. The key point for the purposes of the Crusades is that it was the nobility, not kings, who had the resources and the manpower to fight in the Holy Land. For this reason, a pope calling a Crusade often had to direct his appeal to the nobles, not the king.

for power and occasionally joined together to force the king's hand on issues that affected them. In England, though (and in Japan), barons (or baronets) occupied the lowest rank of nobility. Frequently, the word *baron* was used to refer to any powerful nobleman, a practice that survived into the twenty-first century in such phrases as "baron of industry."

Another common title found in connection with the Crusades is duke. In England, a duke was a hereditary noble whose rank was directly below that of the king. On the continent of Europe, a duke was the ruler of a duchy, typically a territory that was part of a loose collection of states. Thus, within the larger Holy Roman Empire, a duke ruled Austria, which was therefore a duchy. "Ruled," though, was a relative term. The amount of actual power a duke or any other nobleman held could vary depending on time and circumstances.

In England members of the hereditary nobility ranked as follows, from highest to lowest: duke, marquess, earl, viscount, and baronet. On the Continent, a count was roughly equivalent to a British earl in rank. All of these titles continue to be used in the 2000s. On the European continent they have little governmental meaning and are primarily social titles, but in England the nobility play a political role in the House of Lords in Parliament. Many women hold these titles, and historically women acquired particular titles not through marriage but "in their own right."

Violence

A second important feature of medieval life was that it was violent. Violence could erupt nearly anywhere and was almost a daily fact of life. Capital punishment (execution) of the most brutal kind was commonplace. Again, without the institutions of the Roman Empire, legal arguments frequently were settled not in an organized court system but in battle or through vendettas (feuds) between families that led to murder and bloodshed. In competition for sometimes scarce economic resources—land, crops, livestock, peasants—neighboring estates frequently resorted to the sword. They often had little choice; it was either that or starvation.

The church tried to channel this hostility so that it was not so random. As a guide, it used both the Old and New Testaments of the Bible, Roman law, and the philosophies of early

Violence and the Medieval Church

Even the church accepted violence as a fact of life, as the following story illustrates. A French knight prayed at a local monastery that God would allow him to avenge his brother's murder by capturing the murderer. Later, the knight and his companions ambushed the victim, mutilated his face, cut off his hands and feet, and castrated him. The knight believed that he had been successful because of divine help, so in gratitude he donated the victim's blood-stained armor and weapons to the monastery where he had prayed. It would seem incredible today, but the monks gratefully accepted them.

church fathers such as Saint Augustine. It developed a belief system that justified warfare in some circumstances. In the eyes of the church, violence was acceptable or not based on the morality (virtue) of the goal to be achieved. Also considered was the state of mind of the persons responsible for the violence. The church saw the goal of saving the Holy Land as good, so it also saw the violence that accompanied the Crusades, violence of the worst and most brutal kind, as defensible. Some of this violence took place on the way to the Crusades. Often it was directed at Jewish communities in Germany and elsewhere, where Crusaders slaughtered innocent people in the belief that they were carrying out God's will (see Chapter 8). Often it was directed against Muslims, such as when the Crusaders slaughtered the Muslim inhabitants of Jerusalem at the end of the First Crusade (see "The Massacre" in Chapter 6).

Knighthood

Knights as we know them—horse-mounted, armored soldiers—first appeared on the scene in about the eighth and ninth centuries. While horses had been used in war before then, soldiers usually dismounted in combat because they could fight more effectively on foot. Then the stirrup was developed, allowing the soldier to remain on horseback and keep his balance. The advantage of being mounted was that the knight could brace himself on horseback while he charged his enemy with a lance. At the time, this was a powerful military innovation, or improvement (see Chapter 10 for a discussion of the equipment and weapons of a typical knight).

Training for knighthood began at an early age. Boys as young as seven were sent to serve as pages, or personal attendants, for a wealthy relative or lord. There they would be trained in using weapons and handling a horse. Part of the training

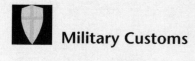

Military Customs

The modern-day military has customs that began during the Middle Ages. One is the salute. After full suits of metal armor came into use, knights could not easily identify one another as friend or enemy because visors (the fronts of helmets) covered their faces. The visor, though, could be raised and lowered. One knight would commonly greet another by raising his hand, holding it flat, and using the tips of his fingers to lift the visor so that the other could recognize him. Today's salute mirrors this gesture.

The other custom is that an enlisted soldier is expected to walk on the left side of an officer, just as a squire did hundreds of years ago. As a knight's shield bearer, the medieval squire walked to his left so that the knight, who typically bore his sword or lance in his right hand (most people are right-handed), would be better able to quickly take his shield from the squire in his left hand.

might include a period of apprenticeship. As an apprentice, the young knight served as a squire (assistant) for an older knight, helping him with his horse or in putting on his armor.

Once the young man's training was finished, usually between the ages of sixteen and twenty, he would be ceremonially knighted and swear an oath of fealty, or loyalty, to his lord. He also committed himself to a host of rituals and vows that made knighthood a kind of fraternity, or a brotherly group. The knight was now bound to his lord and had to serve for a fixed period of time, typically four years. During peacetime, he was expected to practice his skills as a knight. He did this with other knights through competitive tournaments, but these tournaments frequently turned into disorderly brawls that resulted in senseless injury and death. Later, kings and the church developed more orderly jousting tournaments, with individual events, to minimize this bloodshed. These jousting tournaments, in which a knight would compete against another knight for the honor of his lady love, became a common feature of life late in the medieval period.

Knights, the Crusades, and chivalry

Until the time of the First Crusade, knights fought entirely for their lords. The Crusades changed that, however.

Two women jousting. Not only did knights participate in jousting tournaments, but so did some women.
Reproduced by permission of The British Library (Royal 2 B. VII).

To conduct the war to reclaim the Holy Land, Pope Urban II and his successors needed the support of nobles and their knights. In fact, Urban always intended that primarily knights, rather than commoners and peasants, would "take up the cross" (referring to the cross on which Christ died) to invade the Middle East and reclaim its holy sites for Christianity. With the support of bishops, priests, and monks across Europe, the "Christianization" of knights began, and thousands of young men embraced the cause. The sword was now also a symbolic cross of Christ.

Joining a Crusade was a way for these men to reconcile, or bring together, two conflicting demands made by two different "lords." On the one hand, their earthly lords required them to fight, kill, and plunder. That was their job. Their lord in heaven, though, the lord of the New Testament, required them to "turn the other cheek" and lead a life of meekness, or humbleness. By becoming a Crusader, the church said, a knight could satisfy the demands of his earth-

or ligūta lacrois por lacorde de soie,
olmit qāt lacroise engenoilō se ploie.
ainte crois ora degi soit tote goie.

ly master while also serving his lord in heaven. More than ever, war was thought of as a glorious adventure, a way to acquire wealth, honor, and prestige (status) while fighting in the name of God and the church against those who did not accept God's word.

A monk giving a crucifix to a knight leaving for the Crusades. *©Archivo Iconografico, S.A./Corbis. Reproduced by permission.*

The code of chivalry

As the pope's warriors, knights were bound by a code of honor, the code of chivalry. Each knight had to swear that he would defend the weak, the poor, widows, orphans, and the oppressed. He was to be courteous, especially to women; brave; loyal to his leaders; and concerned about the welfare of his subordinates, or those of lesser rank and position. Quoted by Grant Uden, in *A Dictionary of Chivalry,* the knight's code of conduct was fixed in a knightly prayer carved in stone at the cathedral of Chartres in France, one that expresses the chivalric ideal:

Most Holy Lord, Almighty Father ... thou who hast permitted on earth the use of the sword to repress the malice [evil] of the wicked and defend justice ... cause thy servant here before thee, by disposing [turning] his heart to goodness, never to use this sword or another to injure anyone unjustly; but let him use it always to defend the just and right.

Similarly, in the late nineteenth century, French scholar Léon Gautier listed, in his book *Chivalry,* what he called the Decalogue (or Ten Commandments) that governed the conduct of a knight under the code of chivalry:

1. Unswerving belief in the church and obedience to her teachings

2. Willingness to defend the church

3. Respect and pity for the weak and steadfastness in defending them

4. Love of country

5. Refusal to retreat before the enemy

6. Unceasing and merciless war against the infidel

7. Strict obedience to the feudal overlord, so long as those duties did not conflict with duty to God

8. Loyalty to truth and to the pledged word

9. Generosity in giving

10. Championship of the right and the good, in every place and at all times, against the forces of evil

To generations of readers, knighthood and chivalry became almost synonymous with, or identical to, respect for and devotion to women, through epic poems and novels such as Sir Walter Scott's *The Talisman* (1825). The following passage from Scott's novel, in which a Scottish Crusader named Kenneth is addressing a Saracen (Muslim), is typical of the chivalric attitude toward women:

Saracen, replied the Crusader, thou speakest like one who never saw a woman worthy the affection of a soldier. Believe me, couldst thou look upon those of Europe, to whom, after Heaven, we of the order of knighthood vow fealty [faithfulness] and devotion, thou wouldst loathe for ever the poor sensual slaves who form thy harem [the women of a Muslim household]. The beauty of our fair ones gives point to our spears, and edge to our swords; their words are our law; and as soon will a lamp shed luster [a glow of light] when unkindled [the fire is put out], as a knight distinguish himself by feats of arms, having no mistress of his affection.

Knightly Orders: The Hospitallers and the Templars

Modern military organizations have small, elite fighting forces that are often called on to carry out the most dangerous and difficult missions. Their long and intense training turns them into finely honed fighting machines. More important, membership in one of these organizations is worn as a badge of honor. Those who earn the honor are thought of as a kind of nobility among a nation's men-at-arms and women-at-arms.

In this respect, little has changed since the Middle Ages. Most knights were born into the nobility. Many of these nobles tended to be drawn to special orders of knighthood, including such organizations as the Knights Hospitallers and the Knights Templars. The nobles who served in these organizations did so for a variety of motives: personal pride, a longing for adventure, and a desire to serve their church. But many also served for economic reasons.

The Crusades were expensive, and the nobles of Europe were the ones who largely paid the bill. This put many of them, particularly minor nobles, under great financial strain. Many lost their estates, either because they spent all of their money helping to fund a Crusade or because they were no longer in Europe to defend their land, or both. Faced with the possibility of financial ruin, many chose to serve in elite units. The chief advantage of doing so was the possibility of financial gain, for these units were funded by kings; the church; and wealthier, higher-ranking nobles. While individual knights in these orders received no payment and, in fact, took priestly vows of poverty, the orders themselves attracted a great deal of money. This gave them power, and that power opened doors for their members and provided ways for them to recover financial losses from taking part in the Crusades.

These medieval knightly orders played an important role in the Crusades. They also featured prominently in the history of the European church in the centuries that followed. The two most famous were the Knights Hospitallers and the Knights Templars.

Knights Hospitallers

The first of these knightly orders was the Knights Hospitallers. The Hospitallers began as a monastic order (monks living in monasteries) known mostly for charitable work, but over time they became more of a military order. They were first formed in the 1070s, before the Crusades, when Jerusalem was under the rule of the Muslims. At the time, pilgrims were arriving daily at the holy city. Many were ill and exhausted from their long journey. With the financial backing of a number of Italian merchants, a knight named Gerard Tenque from the Italian city of Amalfi obtained permission from the Muslims to establish a hospital in connection with the Benedictine monastery dedicated to Saint John the Baptist in Jerusalem. This monastery not only would tend to the sick but also would offer "hospitality" to visitors.

During the turmoil surrounding the First Crusade (1095–99), the Knights Hospitallers left the city. After the fall of Jerusalem to the Crusaders in 1099, they returned and re-opened the hospital to tend to the even greater number of pilgrims who were making the trip. At the organization's

857 Ancien hôpital Saint-Jean à Jérusalem. Palestine

height in the early twelfth century, the Hospitallers could take in up to two thousand visitors per day. Although the order continued to be known as the Knights Hospitallers, the official name of the organization changed after the First Crusade. The monastery had always been dedicated to Saint John the Baptist, so the order became known as the Sovereign Military Order of the Hospital of Saint John of Jerusalem, or simply the Knights of Saint John, a name it kept until 1314.

A late 1870s photograph of the Hospital of Saint John of Jerusalem run by the Knights Hospitallers.
Michael Maslan Historic Photographs/Corbis. Reproduced by permission.

After the fall of Jerusalem, pilgrims to the holy city needed military protection along the route. Although the holy city was in the hands of the Crusaders, the route leading to the city, particularly the vast stretches between Christian strongholds, remained full of danger. The Crusader kings lacked enough manpower to patrol these routes and keep them open. So the new master of the hospital, Raymond du Puy, turned the Knights of Saint John into more of a military force, able to drive off or discourage those who would do harm to pilgrims.

The Hospitallers also became a vital source of information to the Crusaders. Many stayed in the region for long periods of time. They formed relationships with Arabs and often learned to speak the language. Their freedom of movement and ties to the local culture made them familiar not only with Christian customs but with local customs and troop movements as well. As they gained power and provided valuable service, their fame spread, and in 1113 they were officially recognized by Pope Paschal II. Then in 1118 they ended their connection with the Benedictine order of monks. Now they gave their allegiance only to the pope and not to kings or other civil rulers.

The Hospitallers consisted of three classes of members. One, the military class, was called the knights of justice; its members had to be of noble birth. These were the warrior-monks, the policemen who kept open the route to the holy city and dreamed of the destruction of Islam. They became part of the West's standing army in the Holy Land and came to regard future Crusaders as mere migrants to the region.

Additionally, there was a class of chaplains, who ministered spiritually to visitors, and a class of brothers, who did the day-to-day work. Honorary members of the order, called *donates* (related to the word "donation"), funded the operation with gifts. The Hospitallers remained heavily dependent on gifts and donations of money and land, leading to the formation of what were called "preceptories" all across Europe. The preceptories were communities that sought members and raised funds for the organization.

Each of the Hospitallers took a monastic vow and lived a hard life. They could be recognized easily by their black robes emblazoned, or decorated, with a large white

cross. For this reason they were frequently referred to as the Knights of the White Cross. While continuing to care for the sick, they also built rest houses, homes for sick and aging knights, and castles used to strengthen the Crusader states. The best known of these castles was called the Krak (sometimes spelled Crac) des Chevaliers, located high on solid rock northeast of the city of Tripoli (in modern-day Lebanon). At around the time of the Third Crusade, the Muslim general Saladin tried to capture the castle, but it was so impenetrable that he failed, and the castle remained in Christian hands until 1271. One of the Hospitallers' chief military contributions during the Crusades was to aid in the capture of the Egyptian-controlled seacoast city of Ascalon, southwest of Jerusalem, in 1153, the last major victory the Crusaders would ever enjoy. Forces of Hospitallers, though, were present at nearly every military engagement, and the order turned into one of the Crusaders' most potent weapons.

The Crusader castle Krak des Chevaliers in Tripoli. It is the best known of the castles built by Knights Hospitallers. *©John J. Jones/Corbis. Reproduced by permission.*

Pilgrims to the Holy Land under the escort of the Knights Templars during the twelfth century. *Private Collection/Ken Welsh/ Bridgeman Art Library. Reproduced by permission.*

After the fall of Jerusalem to the Muslims in 1187, the order moved first to the castle at Margat, east of Tyre (in modern-day Lebanon), and then settled in Acre, a seacoast city north of Jerusalem, in 1189. When Acre fell in 1291, the order moved out of the Holy Land. First it settled on the Mediterranean island of Cyprus, but later it moved to the island of Rhodes and then to the island of Malta in 1530. At this point the order changed its name to the Knights of Malta, the name by which it continues to be known.

In the centuries immediately following the Crusades, the Hospitallers maintained their reputation as warriors. They fought Muslim Turks in the Mediterranean and acted as escorts for pilgrims traveling by sea. But as time went on, their work became entirely charitable rather than military. Perhaps the high point of the Hospitallers came not during the Crusades but in 1783, when a major earthquake hit Sicily. When news reached Malta, the Hospitallers immediately boarded their ships and ferried food and supplies to the ravaged island. Still wearing the black robes emblazoned with the white cross, they sat at the bedsides of the wounded and dying. In modern times the Knights of Malta continue to be known for their charitable and hospital work. In 1926 an association of the Knights of Malta was formed in the United States.

Knights Templars

The Hospitallers won a good deal of fame during the Crusades and survived into the twenty-first century. While they were an important knightly order, they were overshadowed by another more famous and more powerful order, the Knights Templars. To some historians, the history of the Crusades is almost identical with the history of the Templars. Without their help, the Christian communities in the Holy Land probably would not have survived as long as they did. In the early years of the Crusades, the Templars and the Hospitallers acted together. Over time, though, they became rivals, and in the later years of the Crusades, the tension between the two orders even erupted into open conflict. This conflict between the elite guards of the Crusaders weakened the Crusader states and contributed significantly to the ultimate failure of the Crusades.

The Templars were formed in Jerusalem in 1119 by two knights, Hugh des Payens and Godfrey of Saint Omer. Originally, they took the name Poor Knights of Christ. But when King Baldwin of Jerusalem gave the knights a home on the site of the Temple of Solomon (which had been built by the Jews) in Jerusalem, also the site of al-Aqsa Mosque, they took the name Knights of the Temple of Solomon, or Templars ("of the Temple") for short.

The role of the Templars in many respects was similar to that of the Hospitallers. But while the Hospitallers retained somewhat more of a reputation for charitable work, the Templars were fierce, passionate fighters. Like the Hospitallers, their chief role originally was to protect pilgrims journeying to the Holy Land. In time, though, the Templars served a much broader role. When hostilities with Muslim forces erupted, the Crusader kings simply did not have enough regular troops under their command. The Templars became the special forces that supplemented the regular troops and, in fact, did much of the actual fighting. Their numbers were never huge; typically, they put up to about three hundred knights in the field. But their ferocity and skill and, especially, experience—in contrast to newly arriving Crusaders—more than made up for any lack of numbers. They were not afraid to die, either. In the final battle of the Seventh and last Crusade, they lost nearly three hundred knights to the Egyptians, and an equal number were slaughtered at the fall of Acre in 1291.

As they gained power and influence, the Templars also frequently acted as advisers. They sat at council tables and took part in the process of deciding on the best course of action. During the Third Crusade, for example, they counseled against marching on Jerusalem, arguing that it would serve no strategic purpose because of the truce between Richard of England and Saladin. None of the rulers in the Holy Land could afford to offend the Templars. Although the Templars owed no allegiance (loyalty) to those rulers, they went to war for them as conditions dictated. The rulers knew that without the Templars, they would find it impossible to hold at bay the Muslims who surrounded them. The Templars dreamed of the day when they could achieve glory by driving the infidel (unbeliever, that is, anyone who was not a Christian) out of the Holy Land. Many secretly also dreamed of the day when perhaps they could even take over as rulers of the Crusader states.

Some Europeans opposed the formation of military orders within the church. The question of the morality of "warrior-monks" was widely debated, especially in church circles. Those who were against the formation of such orders as the Templars believed that a religious order should emphasize prayer or charitable work. Some even thought that fighting, especially by someone who had taken a monastic vow, was sinful. For these reasons, Bernard of Clairvaux, the same Bernard who preached the Second Crusade, wrote a book in support of the Templars whose Latin title is *De laude novae militiae*, or *In Praise of the New Knighthood.*

Bernard also developed rules for the order, and these orders were severe. The Templars took monastic vows. They were to eat simple meals and sleep together in a single room, fully clothed and ready for action, with candles burning. They were never to gaze at women; if necessary, they were to look at a woman only long enough to identify her. They were allowed no personal property except for three horses, their weapons, and plain dress, notably a white tunic with a red cross. (While the Hospitallers were the Knights of the White Cross, the Templars were the Knights of the Red Cross.) All amusement, including activities such as chess and hunting, was forbidden.

The Templars were given official recognition by Pope Honorius at the church Council of Troyes in 1128. From that point on, they, like the Hospitallers, gave their allegiance only to the pope. Again like the Hospitallers, they received gifts of money and estates, but they attracted more donations, making the order in time immensely powerful and wealthy. The Templars supplemented this wealth by becoming, in effect, bankers in the Holy Land. They made loans and funded merchant activity, often charging very high rates of interest. Many of them learned to speak Arabic, so they not only managed a system of spies but also carried on profitable business activities with the Muslims. The Templars had little trouble recruiting knights from Europe. As the fame of the Templars spread, many knights, especially those who lived on bankrupt estates, were eager to join an order that was growing yearly in power and wealth.

The Templars were composed of three orders. At the top of the hierarchy were the knights themselves, under the control of a grand master. They were usually recruited from the nobility, and only they could wear the white tunic with a red cross. These, of course, were the organization's warriors. Beneath the knights were the sergeants. These men, about five thousand of them, tended to be from the middle classes. Wearing a black tunic with a red cross, they typically served as grooms, or servants, to the knights and often functioned as sergeants at arms. The third class consisted of the clerics, or chaplains. These men carried out religious, medical, and other nonmilitary functions.

The later history of the Templars is as rich as that during the Crusades. After the fall of Jerusalem in 1187, they moved to Acre. With Acre's fall in 1291, they moved to the Mediterranean island of Cyprus. In short order, they abandoned warfare and became the leading money handlers in Europe. Their holdings of land grew, and as they became richer, they served as bankers for such kings as Louis IX of

Friday the Thirteenth

The superstition of Friday the thirteenth may have begun during this purge (elimination) of the Templars. The pope did not want the arrest of the Templars throughout Europe to occur in a piecemeal (fragmented) way. He wanted as many of them as possible rounded up and arrested at the same time, so that they did not have a chance to flee or organize opposition. To that end, he sent out sealed orders to authorities and military commanders throughout Europe, ordering the arrests. The orders were all to be opened and executed on the same date, on Friday, October thirteenth. The ill fortune of the Templars on that day may have given rise to the widely held superstition that Friday the thirteenth is an unlucky day.

France. Because of their power and because, by papal decree, they were not subject to any rulers, they also became hated and feared.

The organization began to come apart in the early fourteenth century. In 1307 King Philip IV of France needed money to go to war against the Flemish. The only place the spendthrift king could get that money was from the Templars. He hated being dependent on an organization that seemed to have as much power as he did (or more), so he launched a persecution of the order. Aided by the pope he had used his power to install, Clement V, he ordered the arrest of all the members of the order. Their property was confiscated (seized by the government), and they were put on trial. Many were tortured to make them confess to charges such as sacrilege (disrespect of holy things), denial of Christ, homosexuality, and satanic worship. In Paris forty-five Templars were burned at the stake in one day.

With the Templars severely weakened, Pope Clement dissolved the order at the church Council of Vienna in 1312. In 1314 the last grand master of the Templars, Jacques de Molay, was burned at the stake. In England, where the Templars operated out of headquarters on Fleet Street, Templar property was seized without violence and handed over to the Hospitallers.

An intriguing question is whether the Templars, in some form, continue to exist as a kind of shadowy, secret cult that pulls hidden levers of financial and political power throughout the world. Many people believe that they do, that their traditions and rituals have been handed down to various secret organizations or societies through the centuries. These organizations are generally referred to under the umbrella name of the Masons or Freemasons. Others believe that the Templars excavated, or dug, under the Church of the Holy

Sepulchre in Jerusalem and discovered secret, mystical knowledge that was the source of their power.

Teutonic Knights

The Teutonic Knights was another knightly order, one that was variously called the Knights of the Virgin Mary or the Teutonic Knights of the Hospital of Saint Mary the Virgin. The order was formed at Acre during the siege of that city in 1190. Like the other orders, the members, who wore a white mantle (robe) with a black cross, took vows of poverty, chastity, and obedience. Their major function was to offer aid to German pilgrims in the Holy Land.

After the Crusades, the Teutonic Knights continued to act as warriors. They turned their attention to fighting the Prussians and other "heathens" in eastern Europe. For many years they held extensive territory under the authority of the pope in such countries as Poland, Russia, and Sweden. In 1809 French emperor Napoleon Bonaparte disbanded the Teutonic Knights, but the order was revived in 1834. The Teutonic Knights, now fully a religious and charitable organization, has its headquarters in Vienna, Austria.

By the end of the Middle Ages, as the technology of war evolved and gunpowder came into use, knights as true warriors were beginning to outlive their usefulness. In the centuries that followed, and still today, knighthood became an honorary institution, granted either by royal decree for service to a nation or to members of civic, fraternal, or charitable organizations.

One historical view of the Crusades emphasizes their brutality, ineffectiveness, religious prejudice, plunder, and mindless bloodshed. Another view emphasizes the Crusades as a stage. On this stage the virtues of piety (devoutness), devotion to a cause, and bravery were enacted by sincere Chris-

Other Chivalric Orders

The history of chivalry through the late Middle Ages continued to witness the formation of knightly orders. These orders were formed for various purposes, and many had colorful names: the Palm and Alligator, the Bee, the Scarf and the Broom Flowers (a reference to the royal family to which Richard I of England belonged, the Plantagenets, a name that means "broom plant"), the Golden Shield, the White Falcon, and even the Fools. Several of these orders consisted of women; the first female knights, according to tradition, fought the Moors (the name given to Muslims on the Iberian Peninsula) in defense of Tortosa, Spain, in 1149.

tians who genuinely believed that their cause was just, as well as by Muslims who were equally committed to their beliefs.

As is frequently the case, the truth lies somewhere between these two views. Although many knights failed to live up to the ideals of the chivalric code, many others did. Like the image of the cowboy in the American Old West, that of the chivalric knight, while often exaggerated, continues to provide a standard of conduct to which many aspire.

For More Information

Books

Finucane, Ronald C. *Soldiers of the Faith: Crusaders and Moslems at War.* London: J. M. Dent, 1983.

Gautier, Léon. *Chivalry.* Edited by Jacques Levron and translated by D. C. Dunning. London: Phoenix House, 1965.

Treece, Henry. *The Crusades.* New York: Random House, 1962.

Uden, Grant. *A Dictionary of Chivalry.* New York: Thomas Y. Crowell, 1968.

War | 10

W hile many common foot soldiers fought and died in the Crusades, the western armies were led by the knights of Europe. Some were kings, such as Richard I of England and Philip II of France. Others were important members of the nobility, including princes, counts, dukes, and barons from countries such as France, Italy, and the Holy Roman Empire. Still others were the nobles' vassals, that is, people under the protection of a lord whom they serve, and lower-ranking knights who were under the vassals' command (see "The Structure of Medieval Society" and "Knighthood" in Chapter 9). As European knights, they would have had similar training, and they would have conducted warfare in similar ways.

The "accoutrements" of a knight

The word *accoutrement* is French and means "equipment." The widespread use of the word among knights at the time reflects the strong influence of France on the Crusades and on knighthood throughout the Middle Ages (roughly 500–1500). Any knight would have taken into bat-

Figure de Philippe Auguste.

Histoire des Rois de France par Dutillet.
Mss. N° 890 de la Bibliothèque Royale.

King Philip II of France led the western armies during the Crusades. *©Stapleton Collection/Corbis. Reproduced by permission.*

tle his "accoutrements" both for defensive and offensive purposes.

Armor

To protect themselves, knights wore armor. The earliest armor, the kind a Crusader would have worn, consisted of chain mail. Chain mail was a kind of fabric made up of thousands of small interlocking metal rings. Its strength protected its wearer from blows from a sword. For this reason, many Muslim warriors fought not only with swords but also with maces, though Europeans used maces too. A mace was a staff with a heavy, spiked metal ball at the end. A horse-mounted Muslim warrior would swing the mace at a Crusader, hoping that the blow would knock him off his horse and that the spikes would penetrate his chain mail and helmet. To ward off such blows, knights carried shields, which were usually made of wood covered with leather.

Helmets with visors (a movable face mask), because they covered the face, made it difficult to identify the wearer in battle, giving rise to what was called "heraldry." Heraldry was a complex system of visual designs used to identify a knight by the noble to whom he owed his allegiance, or loyalty. These symbols also may have served as rallying points during the heat of battle, much like a flag. The symbols consisted of various bars, color schemes, and animals (such as a leopard or lion), as well as a family motto, usually in Latin.

Knights wore these heraldic symbols on their shields and elsewhere, including on their surcoats, or large, sleeveless overcoats worn over the armor. For this reason the symbols came to be called coats of arms. In time, every noble family had its unique coat of arms, a symbol of pride, heritage, and prestige, or status.

As time went on and weapons such as the longbow and crossbow were developed, which many knights viewed as

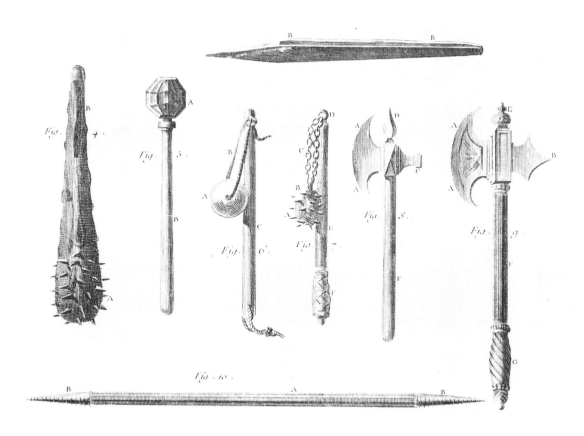

cowardly because they could be used from afar rather than in close combat, chain mail became less effective. For this reason, armor made out of metal plates began to appear in the thirteenth century. Full suits of metal armor, which protected the knight's entire body, did not appear until about the fifteenth century, so the image of the "knight in shining armor" dates to after the Crusades. In the meantime, bows were becoming more accepted among western warriors. Because of its length and strength, the longbow was effective against distant targets. In the twelfth century the church outlawed use of the crossbow as cruel, but knights ignored this law. Crossbows, which were held sideways, aimed like a gun, and shot using a trigger mechanism, were extremely accurate over shorter distances.

Weapons

The knight fought with two standard weapons. One was the lance, which, because of its length, gave the horse-

An illustration of various weapons used during the Crusades. Included are weapons such as lances, maces, and battle-axes. *©Bettmann/Corbis. Reproduced by permission.*

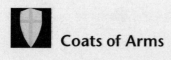

Coats of Arms

Heraldry gave rise to a special vocabulary (including many words from the French), which was almost impossible to understand. A coat of arms might be described, for example, as "argent, a saltire azure, cantoned with four markings of ermine sable." A crest, an identifying emblem of a knight, might be said to have "a lion's head erased azure langued gules." These descriptions, which sound like a foreign language, had meaning to knights in the Middle Ages. They told the knights the colors, designs, pictures, and other features of a coat of arms. In these examples, "azure" is a shade of blue, a "saltire" is an X, "ermine" is a color combination of black spots on a white background, an "erased lion's head" meant that it was cut off, and "langued gules" meant that the lion's tongue was red.

One phrase from medieval heraldry still used in England and often found in English literature is "blot on the 'scutcheon." A 'scutcheon, or escutcheon, is a shield. A knight found guilty of a dishonorable act would suffer an "abatement of honor," and a mark, or "blot," would be placed on his shield, dishonoring him and his family. "Blot on the 'scutcheon" is still used as a figure of speech to refer to a family's dishonor or guilty secret.

mounted knight an advantage over enemies on the ground. The other, of course, was the sword. During the Crusades, the sword began to acquire a strong religious connotation, or association, because it was shaped much like a cross, or crucifix. The very term *Crusade* meant "to take up the cross" in the service of God, and for most knights, the sword was a symbol of the cross on which Christ died. Many knights, especially wealthier ones, carried swords that were elaborately decorated with engravings or encrusted with jewels. While the early Crusaders carried their own swords from Europe, those who stayed in the Middle East came to prefer local swords made with steel from the Syrian city of Damascus. This steel was stronger than the steel made in Europe.

All of the accoutrements of knighthood were a badge of prestige. The mere fact of owning a horse, armor, and a dazzling sword was a sign of wealth and position. But as many European knights learned, the heavy armor and weapons suitable in the cooler climates and on the firmer ground of western and northern Europe were often a nuisance in the extreme heat and desert sands of the Middle

Knights in a sword battle. The sword was one of the standard weapons that knights used. *Reproduced by permission of The British Library (Add. 10294).*

East. These differences between the regions led to differences in fighting styles. Heavily armored Europeans rode powerful stallions, or male horses, that could carry their weight. In battle the Crusaders relied on massed, tightly closed formations. They would simply point their lances forward, bear down on an opposing army, and overwhelm it by brute force. In contrast, the Arab and Turkish Muslims were desert warriors. They rode long-legged, nimble, swift mares, or female horses, and wore no armor that would have weighed them down and made them less mobile in the sand. Their chief tactic in battle was to attack repeatedly and then withdraw, trying to draw their opponents out of formation. They would then quickly retreat, shooting arrows at their opponents with small, tightly strung bows.

One problem both the Crusaders and their opponents occasionally had might seem almost comical today. While Europeans preferred stallions, Arabs and Turks favored mares. At times, especially in the spring, when female horses go into

An interior view of Krak des Chevaliers, one of the most famous Crusader castles. Although many of the Crusaders occupied castles that were already present, in nearly every case the Crusaders strengthened them. *©Elio Ciol/Corbis. Reproduced by permission.*

heat (ready for breeding), the Crusaders' stallions showed more interest in mating with the female horses than in fighting. The Crusaders came to admire the Arabs' swift mares and took a number back to Europe to breed with the stockier horses there. The result was the breed called Thoroughbreds, which are still widely ridden today. All Thoroughbred horses are descended from a relatively few Arabian mares.

Castles, sieges, and siege machinery

Horses, lances, and swords were offensive weapons, used on fields of battle, but equally important was defense, and for defense both the Crusaders and the Muslims relied heavily on castles. Many of the castles the Crusaders occupied were already present when they arrived, but in nearly every case the Crusaders strengthened and expanded them. At the same time, the Crusaders, built many new castles

throughout their kingdoms in the Levant (the European name for the countries on the eastern shore of the Mediterranean). Describing the castle that defended Jerusalem, one pilgrim to the city, quoted by C. N. Johns in an article titled "The Citadel, Jerusalem," wrote in 1106:

> It is curiously built in massive stone, is very high, and of square, solid impregnable [unable to be penetrated] form; it is like a single stone from its base up. It contains plenty of water, five iron gates and two hundred steps to the summit [top]. An immense quantity of corn [grain] is stored in this tower. It is very difficult to take and forms the main defence of the city. It is carefully guarded and no one is allowed to enter except under supervision.

This passage could have described virtually any castle in the Crusader states of Jerusalem, Antioch, Edessa, and Tripoli.

In campaign after campaign, the Crusaders took refuge in castles, often to wait for reinforcements, while their opponents surrounded them. The castles were, in effect, forts,

A medieval battering ram. Weapons such as this were often used during the Crusades to knock down the walls and gates surrounding a city. *©Chris Hellier/Corbis. Reproduced by permission.*

where supplies could be stored and soldiers could find refuge. After the First Crusade, war in the Middle East, from the perspective of the Crusaders, was largely defensive in nature, so the Crusaders learned to make many improvements in the architecture of castles. To better ward off their opponents, they developed such innovations, or improvements, as the overhanging parapet. A parapet is a low wall that defenders crouched behind on the top of the castle's main massive wall, some of which were up to 15 feet (4.5 meters) thick. The overhanging parapet made it easier for them to heave hot oil or to shoot arrows at their attackers below. Another innovation was the angular entryway, which prevented attackers from shooting directly through gates into the castle's interior.

Siege warfare

The chief tactic for capturing an occupied castle or a walled town, which served much the same defensive purpose as a castle, was the siege (from the French word *siége,* meaning "to sit"). An attacking army, whether Christian or Muslim, frequently could do nothing other than camp outside the castle or the city's walls and wait for those inside to surrender. Typically, their goal was to starve the defenders into submission by cutting off supplies, especially food. The more provisions a castle or city had within its walls, the longer it could wait for the invaders to lose patience and leave. Most castles and fortified (strengthened) cities had their own supplies of water and immense caverns that could hold enough food for months, even years. As a result, the besiegers on the outside sometimes ran out of food first.

A well-equipped army, though, was not always willing to wait, so it used "siege engines," or "siege machinery," to gain entry. At the time of the First Crusade, siege engine technology was more highly developed in the East than it was in the West. But Muslim invaders in such places as Spain had used siege machinery, so the Europeans learned from them and were quickly catching up.

Siege engines, which were often built on the spot from materials at hand rather than transported, had at least three functions. One was to batter down walls and gates. The basic engine used for this purpose was the battering ram. Battering rams were typically made of immense poles or tree

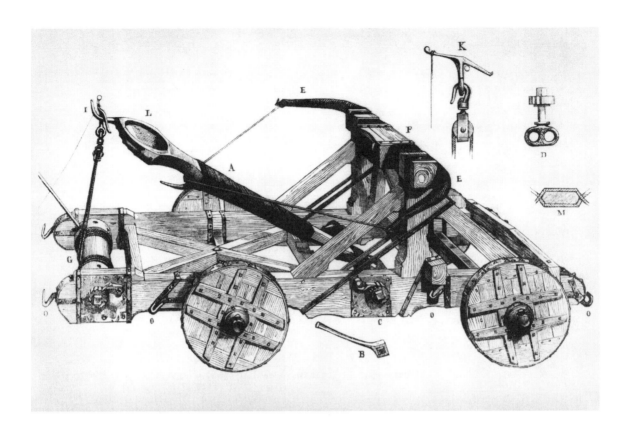

trunks, usually with a metal head. A team of men would rhythmically swing the ram back and forth against a gate until it shattered. Often they had to duck arrows, firebombs, or burning pitch (tar) hurled at them from above.

A second function of siege engines was to allow attackers to scale the walls. A long scaling ladder could be easily made from any materials available. Attackers also used scaling forks, which were long poles with hooks used to snare defenders and pull them off the tops of walls. A more elaborate structure was the belfry, or siege tower. This was a tall, movable tower, similar to scaffolding, from which archers could shoot arrows down into a city or over a castle's walls. If it could be moved close enough to the walls, attackers could use it to climb onto the tops of the walls and gain entrance.

A third function of siege engines was to hurl missiles, such as stones and firebombs, over the walls. They could also be used to practice psychological warfare, or warfare designed

A catapult like the one pictured here was often used during siege warfare to fling beehives, dead and diseased animals, and even the severed heads of captured enemy soldiers and civilians over the walls of the city. *©Christel Gerstenberg/Corbis. Reproduced by permission.*

The Siege of the Castle of Montferrand

A vivid description of siege warfare was provided by William of Tyre, a chronicler who wrote about the Crusades in *A History of Deeds Done beyond the Sea*. Here is a portion of his description of the siege on the castle of Montferrand laid by Turkish general Imad al-Din Zengi in 1137 (for more on Zengi, see "Zengi, Nur al-Din, and Saladin" IN CHAPTER 7).

Meanwhile, Zengi continued his vigorous attacks upon the besieged with unremitting zeal. The very walls shook under the impulse [force] of his mighty engines. Millstones and huge rocks hurled from the machines fell into the midst of the citadel, shattered the houses within, and caused intense fear to the refugees there. Great fragments of rock and all kinds of whirling missiles were hurled with such violence against them that there was no longer any place of security within the walls where the feeble and wounded might be hidden. Everywhere was danger, everywhere hazard [risk], everywhere the spectre [haunting vision] of frightful death hovered before their eyes…. With this very object in view, their cruel foe redoubled [renewed] his assaults.

more to frighten and wear down the enemy than to defeat him. A common tactic, for example, was to fling beehives, dead and diseased animals, and even the severed heads of captured enemy soldiers and civilians over the walls.

The latter types of siege engines were much more elaborate than the others and required more engineering. Typically, crusading armies would have in their ranks builders and engineers who were experts in the craft of designing and constructing these engines. A general name given to many of them, especially those that hurled stones, was perrier, but they came in different types, depending on how they operated.

One type was the mangon, or mangonel, which was made of a long, flexible beam that was pulled down with a rope to create tension. When the rope was released, stones or fire-bombs in a hollowed-out cup at the end of the beam would be hurled through the air. In contrast was the trebuchet, which relied not on tension but on a system of counterweights, boxes of stones or sand dropped down on one end of a beam to propel the missile at the other, similar to the operation of a seesaw. Some of these artillery pieces launched other types of missiles. The ballista, for example, was much like a very large crossbow and could throw metal shafts, like large arrows, as well as stones and fire-bombs. While all these engines were used to project missiles over the walls, they could also be used to pulverize the walls, allowing the attackers to gain entrance. The best siege engines could launch missiles as far as 200 or more yards (183 meters) or could hurl stones weighing up to a quarter ton (227 kilograms).

A final tactic used in siege warfare was undermining, often called sapping. This consisted of burrowing under the walls of a castle or a fortified city. The goal was to weaken the walls so that they would collapse. Frequently, undermining would expose wooden timbers used to support the walls. These would then be set on fire, again causing the walls to collapse. Occasionally, the goal of undermining was to create tunnels, which then could be used to flood the castle if the terrain allowed water to flow down from nearby higher elevations. Sometimes, of course, undermining was not a good option because the castle was built on solid rock. Even then, Muslims often brought forces of miners, in some cases hundreds of them, to bore into the rock.

For More Information

Books

Hoggard, Brian. *Crusader Castles: Christian Fortresses in the Middle East.* New York: Rosen Publishing, 2004.

Kennedy, Hugh. *Crusader Castles.* New York: Cambridge University Press, 1994.

Uden, Grant. *A Dictionary of Chivalry.* New York: Thomas Y. Crowell, 1968.

Verbruggen, J. F. *The Art of Warfare in Western Europe during the Middle Ages, from the Eighth Century to 1340.* Translated by Sumner Willard and R. W. Southern. Rochester, NY: Boydell Press, 1977.

William of Tyre. *A History of Deeds Done beyond the Sea.* 2 vols. Translated by Emily Atwater Babcock and A. C. Krey. New York: Columbia University Press, 1943.

Periodicals

Johns, C. N. "The Citadel, Jerusalem." *Quarterly of the Department of Antiquities in Palestine* 14 (1950): 121–190.

Web Sites

Thomas, Jeffrey L. "Castle Siegecraft and Defence." *Castle of Wales.* http://www.castlewales.com/siege.html (accessed on July 27, 2004).

11 Literature and Song of the Crusades

Throughout its history, literature has passed through two broad stages and is still in a third stage. In each of these stages, poets; playwrights; and, in modern times, novelists tended to write about similar subjects, mostly because these were the subjects that interested their readers or listeners. Ancient literature, for example, the literature of ancient Greece and Rome, tended to focus on the activities of gods and their involvement in human affairs. Modern literature, literature since roughly 1700, has focused more on the day-to-day lives of ordinary people in realistic settings. Between these periods were the Middle Ages (roughly 500–1500), when the most common subject matter of literature was neither gods nor ordinary people, but a class of people who fell between the two, larger-than-life heroes.

Many exceptions to these trends can be found, and it would be impossible to assign firm dates to when these shifts took place, just as it would be impossible for a scientist to say specifically when a species of animal first appeared. Nonetheless, some of the most important literary works throughout history show this evolution from the Age

of the Gods through the Age of Heroes to the Age of Realism in literature.

Heroic literature

Much of the literature of the Middle Ages was "heroic literature." Most of it shared two important features. First, the language used was not the Latin of priests and monks working in their monasteries. Latin was considered the language of educated people in Europe during the Middle Ages. Instead, the literature was composed in the "vernacular" languages, or the everyday languages spoken by people in France, England, Spain, Germany, and the other nations of Europe.

Second, most of this literature was not written down, at least until later, sometimes centuries later. Very often, different versions of a literary work survive. Meanwhile, before the invention of the printing press, most vernacular literature was passed along orally, often by wandering poets and musicians who entertained audiences with stories about their "betters." Many of these stories were legends and tales that already existed. Individual poets often could not read, but they had excellent memories, so they could learn lengthy stories and poems to recite. Generally, each would embellish those stories and poems with new details or new story lines, so that as time went on, the stories grew and expanded. Frequently, the later "writer" of a work was simply recording legends that had been passed along for a long time.

Many different groups populated Europe during the early Middle Ages: the Vikings, the Franks, the Goths, the Saxons, the Magyars, and others. They lived in a bloody and violent age. The virtues that ensured survival were not humility, or meekness, but courage, skill as a warrior, and loyalty to a clan or tribe and its leaders. This was a time when heroic kings and warriors strode across the stage of Europe. It was an age of conquerors, of emperors, of warrior dukes and princes, of knights doing battle against chaos, as Europeans tried to emerge from the backwardness of the Dark Ages (as this time period was sometimes called) and form a civilization.

The epic literature of the early Middle Ages, much of it from German-speaking regions, celebrated the deeds of these great men. The epic poem was typically sung or recited to an audience at feasts and on other occasions. Stories such as *Beowulf* in England or the *Niebelungenlied* in the Scandinavian and Germanic countries preserved the real world and the values of bloody warriors who survived through cunning and strength in a dangerous, brutal age.

As time progressed and the influence of the Christian church grew wider, the values celebrated in the epics came into conflict with the message of Christ found in the biblical New Testament. The church, therefore, tried to impose a different set of values on people. The ideal people for the Christian church were not the blood-soaked warriors, but monks and saints. These people were humble and poor. They rejected the world and focused on a life of the spirit. They lived lives of holiness, and they very often died for their religious faith as martyrs.

By about the tenth and eleventh centuries, many of Europe's warriors were accepting these values. Stories survive of many nobles—dukes, princes, even kings—who entered the church, became monks, and lived lives of prayer and seclusion, or isolation. They cut their hair in the "tonsure," a ring of hair surrounding a bald area, to imitate the crown of thorns placed on Christ's head when he died. Within the church, the most common form of literature was stories celebrating the lives of saints and martyrs.

Then the Christian church began to expand and flex its muscle. Popes became more powerful and had more influence over the people of Europe than their kings did. To the east, the church tried to win converts among the Slavic peoples. Armed Christians resisted the invasion of Islam in Spain and other parts of Europe. Out of this expansion came a new ideal, one that combined the ideals of the epic warrior with those of the saint. This was the Christian warrior, one who mingled deeply held religious faith with a desire to fight for that faith. His sword, with its long blade and crossing hand guard, became a symbol of the cross on which Christ was crucified and died. This development, the Christian knight, flowered during the Crusades. Now warriors were to fight not for territory or to gain vengeance (revenge) against enemies and traitors, as the heroes of the old epics did, but to win souls for their church and their God. The ideal was not the bloody pagan (believer in many gods) warrior of the Germanic epics but someone like a Knight Templar (see Chapter 9), a Christian noble who entered an elite corps of warrior-monks to fight and, if necessary, die for his faith.

The chanson de geste

The literary form called the chanson de geste emerged from this blending of the ideals of the Germanic warrior and the Christian saint. The term is French and means something like "song of deeds," especially heroic deeds, and the chansons de geste typically celebrated heroic deeds of chivalry (see "Knights, the Crusades, and Chivalry" in Chapter 9). They were poems that could be sung or recited. They used simple but vivid (dramatic) language that relied on the poetic device of assonance. (Assonance is a kind of rhyme in which vowel sounds are repeated, so that, for example, "lake" would rhyme not just with "take" but also with "tale.") Like the ear-

A page from *Chanson de Roland,* **or** *The Song of Roland.* **This illustration is of a Crusader army pitching camp.** *Reproduced by permission of The British Library (Lansdowne 782).*

lier epics, they were oral literature, passed along by minstrels and troubadours, medieval musical performers.

The earliest chansons de geste probably were composed in about the ninth or tenth century. The most famous examples of the form came a little later, and many dealt with the life of the Frankish warrior-king Charlemagne, or Charles the Great (742–814). Like many chansons de geste, they were composed in what are called cycles, or separate groupings of poems that look at different parts of Charlemagne's life. Thus, the first group deals with Charlemagne's childhood. The second tells of his efforts to subdue his rebellious vassals (people in service to a lord, who gives them protection). The third treats his battles to extend Christianity to the east. The fourth group deals with his activities before he went off to fight the Moors (or Muslims) in Spain (see "Spanish Islam" in Chapter 1).

La Chanson de Roland

The most famous chanson de geste concerning the life of Charlemagne is contained in the last cycle, which tells of Charlemagne's exploits fighting the Moors in Spain. This poem is called *La Chanson de Roland,* or *The Song of Roland.* The poem, as it survives into the 2000s, most likely was written down around the year 1100, and its probable author was a poet named Turold, who came from Normandy in France. The subject of the poem is the Battle of Roncesvalles in 778, fought as Charlemagne and his army were leaving Spain and crossing the Pyrenees to return to France. In real life the battle was against the Basques, an ethnic group that lived in the region between France and Spain. But *The Song of Roland* turns it into a heroic battle against the "Saracens," as Muslims usually were called in Europe at the time. Ironically, Charlemagne is remembered more for his only defeat than for his many victories, for much of his army was wiped out at the Battle of Roncesvalles.

One who supposedly fell in battle that day was Charlemagne's nephew, Count Roland. He and his troops were the victims of the treachery of Roland's stepfather, Ganelon. Roland had proposed that Ganelon be sent to negotiate peace terms with the Saracens. Ganelon was angry with Roland because the mission was so dangerous. In his anger, he conspired with the Saracens to lay a trap for Roland, who led the rearguard of Charlemagne's army and was ambushed at the mountain pass at Roncesvalles.

According to the legend, Roland was one of the so-called Twelve Paladins, or close advisers to the king. Roland, however, may not have existed, though he may have been based on an actual person. As the story of the Battle at Roncesvalles spread and grew throughout the rest of the Middle Ages, the name of Roland became renowned. Minstrels and troubadours added freely to the legend. Throughout Europe, people knew of Roland's sword Durandal, his trusty horse Veillantif, and the horn of Roland, which he blew to lead troops into battle.

Of course, other chansons de geste were written as well, and some of them had to do directly with the Crusades. One is called the *Chanson d'Antioch,* or *Song of Antioch,* and focuses on the siege of Antioch in 1097, during the First Crusade (1095–99; see "The First Crusade" in Chapter 6). It probably was written by an eyewitness to the siege, Richard the Pilgrim, but it was reworked later by a French writer, Graindour de Douai.

Lyrics of courtly love

Another type of literature that evolved during the time of the Crusades was poetry that dealt with courtly love. (Courtly love referred to the "code," or "rules" lovers followed at court.) In France the sources of many of these poems were two separate but related groups of singer-poets. The best known today were the troubadours, who flourished in the southern regions of France, especially Provence, as well as in northern Spain and northern Italy. Many of these poets were knights. The other group were the *trouvères,* who flourished more in northern France. While both groups sang of courtly love, the songs of the *trouvères* tended to be more satirical, or humorous and mocking. A third group, called the Minnesängers, sang of courtly love in the German-speaking regions.

The inspiration behind this form of poetry came from the Arab Muslims (followers of the Islamic faith), both in Spain and in the Middle East at the time of the Crusades. While earlier Christian thinking had seen women as the fallen daughters of the biblical Eve and regarded sex as an animal instinct, the Arabs looked at women with more of a sense of worship. The

Crusaders took this viewpoint back to Europe. One of the sponsors of a great deal of courtly love poetry was Eleanor of Aquitaine, who accompanied her husband, King Louis VII, on the Second Crusade, which began in 1146. Many of these poems of courtly love dealt with the theme of a knight leaving his ladylove as he went on Crusade.

Courtly love poetry described the intense emotions and the codes of behavior followed by lovers at court. According to the conventions, or "rules," of the poems, the purpose in life of the courtly lover was to serve his lady. Most of the time, the love affairs in the poems were adulterous, that is, they were relationships outside marriage. This was because most marriages among the nobility were economic and political arrangements and were not based on love. In many other poems, the lover saw his lady as an ideal person whose hand he could

Eleanor of Aquitaine (right) was a great sponsor of courtly love poetry during the Crusades.
©Bettmann/Corbis.
Reproduced by permission.

never hope to win. The courtly lover saw himself as serving the god of love and worshiping his lady, whom he viewed as a saint. The greatest sin that a courtly lover could commit was faithlessness to his ladylove.

In time, the traditions of courtly love came to be part of much of the literature of the medieval period. One of the great long poems of the late Middle Ages, *The Divine Comedy*, by the Italian poet Dante (written from about 1310 to 1314), relies on courtly love traditions. The speaker of the poem is inspired by his earthly lover, Beatrice, who serves as his guide to Paradise, or heaven. Even later, in the late sixteenth century, Shakespeare's Romeo sums up the traditions of courtly love when he sees Juliet on the balcony and says, "It is my lady. O, it is my love."

Romance

A final literary form from the late medieval period was the romance. This form combined the traditions of the

An Example of a Courtly Love Lyric

Here is a very brief example of courtly love poetry, a short poem written in the tradition of the German Minnesängers. (*Minne-* means something like "ideal love.") The German version is above the English translation. Interestingly, this poem, found by Gundrata Sidricsdottir and quoted in the Edinburgh University Medieval Society newsletter, *Feudalist Overlord,* was written in the margin of a Bible, apparently by a monk to a nun. The letter shows that the impulses of courtly love were not restricted to laypersons:

Du bist min, ich bin din,

des solt du gewis sin,

du bist beslozen in minem herzen,

verlorn ist daz sluzzelin,

danne muost du ouch iemer darinne sin.

(You are mine, I am yours,

you should be sure of this,

you are locked up in my heart,

the little key is lost,

so you must always be inside it.)

chansons de geste and of courtly love lyrics. From the chanson de geste they took the theme of the crusading knight who performed noble and heroic deeds while on a quest of some sort. But his search is for an ideal that he can never attain, or achieve, just as the lady of courtly love lyrics was often beyond reach. Reaching the goal was not as important as the quest itself, the striving for something higher and nobler in life. Romances had many elements that today would be called "romantic," but the word "romance" in this context always refers to vernacular languages, such as French and Spanish. These were languages that came from southern Europe and the region around Rome. Although German is not a Romance language, many romances came from German-speaking countries.

The topics of romances were still heroes, usually heroic knights. Many treated what was called the "Matter of Britain." This referred to all the tales and legends surrounding England's King Arthur and the Knights of the Round Table. These stories originated on the British Isles among the people called Celts, but in time they became immensely popular throughout Europe. Sometimes romances treated the "Matter of Antiquity," meaning heroes connected with an-

cient cities such as Troy. Finally, the "Matter of France" referred to stories surrounding Charlemagne.

These stories, though, were not like the old epics, nor were they quite like the chansons de geste. The epics were bloody and violent. Mere survival against the forces of chaos was the major goal. The focus of the chansons de geste was heroic deeds. The later medieval romances, in contrast, focused more on the efforts of heroes to make themselves better people or to gain spiritual insight, usually by taking part in a quest. The goal of this quest was often a sacred object, and one of the most commonly sought-after sacred objects was the Holy Grail, generally regarded as the cup that Christ drank out of during the Last Supper. The Grail, however, was a symbol for a higher ideal. This emphasis on the search for a relic, or a holy object, of Christ grew in part out of the efforts of the Crusaders to preserve the holy sites of Palestine and Jerusalem, particularly the tomb of Christ, and relics of the True Cross on which Christ was crucified.

graal.er.j.home as potences.

A page from *Perceval; or, The Story of the Grail,* in which the title character embarks on a quest to find the Grail. In this scene knights carry a silver case containing the Holy Grail to France. *©The British Library/Topham-HIP/The Image Works.*

In France one of the major writers of romances was Chrétian de Troyes, who wrote primarily from about 1165 to 1180. Largely during these years, he wrote five major romances, all drawing on the Matter of Britain. *Erec* tells the story of a wife who shows her love for her husband by disobeying his commands. *Cligès* is a love story about an unhappy wife who fakes her own death and comes back to life to enjoy happiness with her lover. *Lancelot* was the name of one of King Arthur's knights, who is a slave to love and to his mistress, Arthur's wife, Guinevere. *Yvain* tells of a widow's marriage to the man who killed her husband. Finally, and perhaps the most important of Chrétian de Troyes's works, was *Perceval; or, The Story of the Grail.*

In *Perceval; or, The Story of the Grail* the title character embarks on an adventurous quest to find the Holy Grail. This story became the basis for *Sir Gawain and the Green Knight,* a well-known fourteenth-century English poem. Much of this material became more familiar to English readers in the fifteenth century and after through Sir Thomas Malory's famous *Le morte d'Arthur,* or *The Death of Arthur,* which tells the entire story of Arthur's life and death. It is from Malory that most English readers are familiar with Arthur and Guinevere; the adulterous relationship between Guinevere and Lancelot; Merlin the magician; the Knights of the Round Table; and Arthur's famous sword, Excalibur.

The Holy Grail and the search for it have always been a source of fascination. To many, possession of the Grail would be a source of great mystical power. Writers and historians have had different views of what the Grail even was or what it represented. One suggestion, advanced in a long poem by German writer Wolfram von Eschenbach, called *Parzival,* was that it was a stone from heaven that provided spiritual rebirth. Wolfram, who wrote his epic between 1200 and 1210, claimed that one of the major sources for his poem was a Crusader named Philip, who was the duke of Flanders and had been in Palestine in 1177.

To some, though, the Grail is not even a physical object. Since the Grail held wine that Christ had transformed into his blood at the Last Supper (a ritual that forms a major part of the Catholic Mass), there are theories that the "Grail" is actually Christ's bloodline, or blood descendants. Some historians believe that the Knights Templars, the order of warrior-monks that played a major role in the Crusades, excavated beneath the site of the Temple of Solomon in Jerusalem (see "Judaism" in Chapter 1) and there discovered the "Grail." But what they discovered was that the Grail referred to royal bloodlines and that earlier French kings were the descendants of Christ. Possession of this knowledge, at least according to legend, was the source of the order's immense power, and it was because of this power that the Templars were destroyed by Pope Clement V in the early fourteenth century (see "Knights Templars" in Chapter 9). Some of these theories are unlikely, but they grow out of traditions of mysticism that many Christians and Jews believed in during the Middle Ages.

The Crusades inspired literature not only in the West but in the East as well. After the conclusion of the First Crusade, a poet named Abu l'Muzaffar al-Abiwardi urged Islam to unite to drive out the Crusaders. His poem, quoted by Francesco Gabrielli in *Arab Historians of the Crusades,* was typical of the type of call to arms issued by poets in the region, particularly as it became clear that the Crusaders were not leaving. Al-Abiwardi wrote:

We have mingled blood with flowing tears, and there is no room left in us for pity.

To shed tears is a man's worst weapon when the swords stir up the embers [glowing fragments from a fire] of war.

Sons of Islam, behind you are battles in which heads rolled at your feet.

Dare you slumber in the blessed shade of safety, where life is as soft as an orchard flower?

This is war, and the man who shuns [avoids] the whirlpool to save his life shall grind his teeth in penitence [regret].

This is war, and the infidel's sword is naked in his hand, ready to be sheathed again in men's necks and skulls.

For More Information

Books

Gabrielli, Francesco. *Arab Historians of the Crusades*. Translated by E. J. Costello. London: Routledge and Kegan Paul, 1969.

Gaunt, Simon. *Retelling the Tale: An Introduction to Medieval French Literature*. London: Duckworth, 2001.

Gerritsen, Willem P., and Anthony G. van Melle, eds. *Dictionary of Medieval Heroes: Characters in Medieval Narrative Traditions and Their Afterlife in Literature, Theatre and the Visual Arts*. Translated by Tanis Guest. Woodbridge, U.K.: Boydell and Brewer, 1998.

Melin, Claude. *Chansons de Gestes*. Paris: Éditiones Alternatives, 1998.

Menocal, Maria Rosa. *The Arabic Role in Medieval Literary History: A Forgotten Heritage*. Philadelphia: University of Pennsylvania Press, 1987.

Web Sites

Sidricsdottir, Gundrata. "Feudalist Overlord: Letter from the Abbess of Reading Abbey." *Edinburgh University Medieval Society* (January–February 2003). http://www.lothene.org/feudalist/abbess.html (accessed on July 27, 2004).

"The Song of Roland: Verses I–LXXXVII." *The Online Medieval and Classical Library*. http://sunsite.berkeley.edu/OMACL/Roland/r1-87.html (accessed on July 27, 2004).

End of the Crusades: Mongols, Mamluks, and Muslims

12

By the middle of the thirteenth century the situation in the Middle East had grown completely chaotic. The Seljuk Empire, which ruled over western Asia, was beginning to fall apart, and in 1244 a new clan of Muslim Turks, the Khwarismians, sacked Jerusalem, leaving few Christian survivors. The remaining Franks (as Crusaders in the Middle East were called) tried to form an alliance with the Syrian Muslims to drive the Turks out, but the Turks decisively defeated a combined Crusader-Syrian army in the Battle of Harbiyah in October 1244. These events triggered the Seventh Crusade, which began in the summer of 1248 and ended with the defeat of King Louis IX of France in 1250 (see "The Seventh Crusade" in Chapter 6).

The invasion of the Mongols

To understand events in the decades following the Seventh Crusade, it is necessary to go back to a time before that Crusade. As he was preparing for the Crusade in the late 1240s, Louis IX was looking for allies in his fight against the Muslims. One potential ally was the Assassins, the western

Scenes on a candlestick showing a Muslim hunting on a horse with a bow and arrow. Artwork like this was being created by Muslims toward the end of the Crusades era. *The Art Archive/Museum of Islamic Art Cairo/Dagli Orti. Reproduced by permission.*

term for a Shiite Muslim sect, or subgroup, called the Ismailis. The Ismailis opposed the orthodox, or mainstream, Sunni Muslims who ruled Islam from Baghdad (see "The Assassins" in Chapter 5). The Assassins' opposition to Sunni Islam was so deep that they often formed alliances with the Christian Franks. But the Assassins were a fanatical (passionate and dedicated) sect that could offer little real help. The eventual fall of Baghdad and the Baghdad caliphate (the dominion of an Islamic leader) in 1258 ended the Ismaili movement (see Chapter 7 on the Cairo/Baghdad caliphate split).

A more promising ally was a tribe of warlike Asians called the Tatars, or Mongols, who were sweeping westward in the thirteenth century and driving out the Seljuks. Years earlier the Mongols had been led by a ruthless general, the famed Genghis Khan, who had begun invading Turkish territories as early as 1219. For Louis, the chief attraction of the largely pagan Mongols was that they were not Muslims; instead, they worshiped many gods. Louis believed that he could convert them to Christianity and forge an alliance with them; together they could defeat Islam. He held this belief in part because some Mongols were already Eastern Orthodox Christians. They were descended from the Eastern Orthodox patriarch of Constantinople, who had been driven out by the Romans in the fifth century and had settled in Asia.

The king had sent ambassadors to the Mongols before the Seventh Crusade. The ambassadors returned in 1247 and reported that the Mongols expressed some interest in an alliance but were more interested in capturing territory. Such an alliance, they suggested, would distract the Muslims, making it easier for the Mongols to attack Muslim-held territory. Then, in 1248, Mongol ambassadors visited Louis as he was docked at Cyprus (an island south of Turkey in the Mediterranean) to make preparations for the Seventh Crusade. These ambassadors said that the Mongols were willing to help the Christians free Jerusalem from Muslim control. In another round of negotiation, Louis sent to the Mongols an ambassador named William of Rubruck, who was en route during the Seventh Crusade. Meanwhile, the pope, too, had sent an ambassador to Asia to conduct discussions with the Mongols.

William returned with disappointing news. The Mongols, he said, showed no interest in converting to Christianity. Worse, they accepted gifts that Louis had sent as "tribute" (payment) from him and referred to him as their new "vassal" (a person in service to a lord). Louis's strategy had fallen apart. It is quite possible that if Louis had not insisted that the Mongols convert to Christianity, he might have won a powerful ally in them. Louis, though, was known for his extreme religious piety (he was made a Catholic saint at the end of the century). So strong was his resistance to an alliance with non-

©Archivo Iconografico, S.A./Corbis. Reproduced by permission.

Christians that he missed a chance to defeat the Muslims and, quite possibly, restore Jerusalem to Christian control. On the other hand, the Mongols were driven solely by the desire for territorial conquest. Historians can only speculate about what the effects of a Christian-Mongol alliance would have been.

Louis stayed in Outremer (the Europeans' term for "the land overseas," or the Christian colonies in the Middle East) for four years after the end of the Seventh Crusade. During that time he strengthened the fortresses at some of the remaining Crusader-held cities, including Acre, Tyre, Jaffa, and Sidon. He also tried to stop the ongoing quarreling among the Crusader barons over territory and succession to thrones. Finally, though, he had to return to France.

After Louis left Outremer in 1254, a state of near civil war prevailed in Acre (in modern-day Lebanon). Merchants from Venice and Genoa, Italy, were openly fighting for their commercial interests in the city. The Knights Hospitallers supported the Genoese, while the Knights Templars supported the Venetians (see "Knightly Orders: The Hospitallers and the Templars" in Chapter 9), and sometimes fighting between the two orders of knights erupted. Few gave thought to freeing Jerusalem or the tomb of Christ, except for Louis. For thirteen years he remained obsessed with his failure to recapture Jerusalem. In 1267 he announced that he was going to return to the Holy Land, and he departed in July 1270 for what is sometimes called the Eighth Crusade. He never arrived. Along the way, an outbreak of disease struck Louis's Crusader force, and in August, Louis died.

The Mongols, meanwhile, under a khan (king) named Hulagu, were making deeper inroads into the Middle East. They had already attacked in Poland and Hungary, and in 1243 they had defeated the Seljuks in Anatolia (a region in western Turkey). They took most of Persia in 1256 and captured Baghdad in 1258, ending the Baghdad caliphate (see "Response to the First Crusade" in Chapter 7). All of Europe rejoiced, for Baghdad was the capital of the Islamic empire. The Crusaders could very well have marched on Jerusalem with success, but as noted earlier, they were too divided among themselves to take advantage of the opportunity the Mongols had given them. Meanwhile, in Syria, the Mongols captured the Syrian cities of Aleppo and Damascus in 1258, breaking the back of the Seljuks.

The Mamluks

Even with their victories, the Mongols had not satisfied their desire for empire and territory. After gaining control of Syria, they set their sights on Egypt. Hulagu sent an ambassador to Cairo, who demanded that Egypt submit.

Tomb of the Mamluks, slave soldiers during the Crusades who fought to win political control of several Muslim states.
©Bettmann/Corbis.
Reproduced by permission.

But by this time military power in Egypt was in the hands of a group called the Mamluks (sometimes spelled Mameluks). The Mamluks were a select fighting force of Turks. They had all been seized as children and raised as Muslims under strict military discipline. Not knowing their real fathers, all were given the name Ibn Abdullah, meaning "son of Abdullah," referring to the father of Muhammad, the founder of the Islamic faith in the seventh century. As the personal bodyguards of the Egyptian sultan (the king of a Muslim state), the Mamluks were trained to give the individual sultan they served their undivided loyalty. Accordingly, when a sultan died, all of his Mamluk warriors were replaced.

During the Seventh Crusade the sultan of Egypt was deposed, or removed from power, by Saif al-Din Qutuz. Before Qutuz could replace the Mamluks, they came to realize that they were a powerful force in their own right and did not need to be replaced. They were a military force looking

for someone to fight, and the rise of the Mongols now gave them an enemy. Qutuz, too, knew that he faced a threat from the Mongols, so he made no effort to replace his Mamluk guard and, in fact, became their commanding general. With no intention of submitting to Hulagu, he and the Mamluks killed Hulagu's ambassador in Cairo and in 1260 marched through Crusader-held territory to take on the Mongols. The Crusaders were content to watch.

Modern houses built on the remains of a Crusader castle. Ruins such as these are all that remain of the Crusades era. *©Roger Wood/Corbis. Reproduced by permission.*

Behind Qutuz's rise to power was one of his Mamluk guards, Baybars, who himself had risen to power through a series of political assassinations, or murders. Baybars helped Qutuz become sultan, and together the two marched on the Mongols. At the Battle of Ain Jalut in 1260, Baybars pretended to attack the Mongols and then retreated. The Mongols pursued him and galloped into an ambush laid by the main body of Mamluks. The Mongol army was destroyed, ending the Mongol threat to Islam.

Baybars asked the sultan to make him governor of Aleppo as a reward. The sultan, suspicious of Baybars's ambition, refused, so Baybars assassinated him, marched into Cairo, and proclaimed himself sultan. Firmly in control of Egypt, he then marched on Aleppo and Damascus, easily capturing those cities. Now the Mamluks, not the Mongols or the Muslims, were in control of Syria.

The end of the Crusader states

With Baybars, more formally known as Rukn al-Din Baybars Bunduqdari, in control of Egypt, the Crusaders were doomed. In 1265 he marched on Caesarea (the old Roman capital of Palestine), captured the city, and destroyed it. He then took the cities of Haifa and Arsuf (in present-day Israel). In 1266 he marched on the Crusader castle at Safed (often spelled Saphet), one of the last strongholds of the Knights Templars, near the Sea of Galilee. The Templars surrendered when they were told that they could escape safely to Acre, but the treacherous Baybars had them all beheaded. The Mamluks then marched on Toron, on the coast, while another Mamluk force moved on Cilicia (a region of Turkey). Along the way the Mamluks killed every Christian they encountered.

By this time all that remained of the Christian kingdoms on the Levant (the countries on the eastern shore of the Mediterranean) were Acre, Jaffa, Antioch, Tripoli, and a few other small towns. Baybars moved on Acre in 1267, but the town was heavily fortified, so he agreed to a truce. It was at this point that Louis IX in France tried to mount an Eighth Crusade to rescue the city. Meanwhile, the Venetian merchants in the city were selling supplies to Baybars, including timber and iron from Europe that he could use to build siege

Baybars's Note to Bohemond

When Baybars destroyed Antioch, its Christian ruler, Bohemond, was away in Tripoli. Baybars sent him the following letter, quoted by Francesco Gabrieli in *Arab Historians of the Crusades,* gloating about his victory:

> Our purpose here is to give you news of what we have just done, to inform you of the utter catastrophe that has befallen you.... You would have seen your knights prostrate [face down] beneath the horses' hooves, your houses stormed by pillagers and ransacked by looters.... You would have seen the crosses in your churches smashed, the pages of the false Testaments [the Bible] scattered, the Patriarchs' tombs overturned. You would have seen your Moslem enemy trampling on the place where you celebrate the mass, cutting the throats of monks, priests and deacons upon the altars.... Since no survivor has come forward to tell you what happened, we have informed you of it.

engines (see "Siege Warfare" in Chapter 10). Not to be outdone, the Genoese merchants were selling slaves to Baybars.

With Acre under a truce, Baybars marched on Jaffa in 1268. After a siege that lasted just twelve hours, he entered the city and destroyed it. He then turned to Antioch, the richest of the Crusader states, where his forces looted the city and butchered every Christian he found. Equipped with massive siege machines, he then took a major Crusader castle, the Krak des Chevaliers, that had resisted siege attempts since the Third Crusade.

The fall of Acre

By now, the only city of any importance that remained in Christian hands was Acre. Baybars, though, died in 1277, so the final Mamluk attack on the city was delayed for fourteen years. In 1285 Baybars's successor as sultan of Egypt, al-Mansur Qalawun, instead captured the last outpost of the Knights Hospitallers, the castle at Margat (sometimes spelled Marqab). He then laid siege to Tripoli, which he captured in 1289.

Few in Europe cared about this development, for Europeans, in general, were sick of crusading. The surviving

Mongols in the region sent an ambassador to the king of England, Edward I. They proposed an alliance against Qalawun, but Edward was busy fighting the Scots in his own realm. King Philip IV of France, too, showed no interest. The pope sent a force of Italian Crusaders in 1290, but their presence proved to be a disaster. Qalawun had signed another truce with Acre and may very well have decided to leave the city alone, but the Italian Crusaders were not interested in truces. They had come to kill Muslims. One day most of them became drunk, and they butchered a number of Muslim farmers who were bringing their crops to the market in Acre. The barons of Acre were furious, but the damage had been done.

Qalawun vowed revenge. He massed his army to march on the city, but he never lived to get his revenge, for on the way to Acre he died. His son, al-Ashraf Khalil, promised to do what his father had intended. To that end, he assembled an overwhelming military force—sixty thousand cavalry, one hundred sixty thousand foot soldiers, and an impressive collection of siege engines. Meanwhile, the Crusaders tried to fortify the city and shipped out women, children, and the elderly. Remaining in the city were about a thousand knights, fourteen thousand foot soldiers, and some thirty thousand citizens.

The siege of Acre began on April 6, 1291. It continued for six weeks, as al-Ashraf's men rained missiles and fire-bombs down on the city and one by one destroyed the towers that defended it. Some of their siege engines could hurl missiles weighing a quarter ton. On May 18 al-Ashraf launched a general assault and seized the city. The scene was eerily like the one that had taken place on July 15, 1099, when the Crusaders had entered Jerusalem at the end of the First Crusade and butchered the city's Muslims. Now, in the last battle, the Muslims massacred Acre's Christians. All of the Templars defending the city, some three hundred, were beheaded. The city was then destroyed.

All that remained of the Crusader presence was a Templar castle at the town of Ruad, which held out for twelve years. The Crusades, though, had ended at Acre, and all that remained to mark where they had been were heaps of rubble. In the fourteenth and fifteenth centuries, talk circulated in Europe of mounting a new Crusade, but little came of it. The Christian rulers of Cyprus retained the title king of Jerusalem, and one, Peter I, managed to gather a European force that attacked Alexandria, Egypt, in 1365. His goal was to capture the city and trade it for Jerusalem. His knights, however, looted the city and returned home. In 1396 King Sigismund of Hungary tried to lead a Crusade, but his army was slaughtered by Turks before it got out of Bulgaria. In 1458 Pope Pius II called a Crusade and even "took the cross" himself, but he died before he could act on his vow. Because these last attempts failed, the Crusades are said to have officially ended in 1291. Nearly two hundred years of bloodshed had finally come to an uneasy finish.

For More Information

Books

Forey, Alan. "The Military Orders, 1120–1312." *The Oxford Illustrated History of the Crusades*. Edited by Jonathan Riley-Smith. New York: Oxford University Press, 2001.

Gabrieli, Francesco. *Arab Historians of the Crusades*. Translated by E. J. Costello. London: Routledge and Kegan Paul, 1969.

Hamilton, Franklin. *The Crusades*. New York: Dial Press, 1965.

Mayer, Hans Eberhard. *The Crusades*. 2nd ed. Translated by John Gillingham. New York: Oxford University Press, 1988.

Web Sites

Dafoe, Stephen. "The Fall of Acre—1291." *Templar History Magazine* 1, no. 2 (Winter 2002). http://www.templarhistory.com/acre.html (accessed on July 27, 2004).

Consequences and Associations of the Crusades

13

Almost exactly two centuries after the fall of Acre, the last Christian stronghold in the East, in 1291—an event that signaled the end of the Crusades—three important events took place in Spain. These events in 1492 could be said to mark the end of the Middle Ages in Europe. That year, King Ferdinand and Queen Isabella finally drove Muslims out of the Iberian Peninsula (Spain and Portugal) after defeating them at their last stronghold, the city of Granada. Also that year, Christopher Columbus began his voyage in search of a westward route to Asia. His voyage launched an age of discovery and exploration that transformed the world, although that transformation had already begun at the time of the Crusades. Finally, Spain offered its Jews an ultimatum: become Christian or leave the country. While many converted under pressure, many others left, and these exiles once again began a search for a homeland. Each of these events reflected long-term outcomes of the Crusades.

Ferdinand and Isabella drive the Muslims out of Granada

From a military standpoint, the Crusades were an utter failure, at least after 1099. What began with high idealism and religious zeal (enthusiasm) quickly turned into a scramble for money and power. The European Crusaders were often brave, but they were just as often vicious, cruel, and stupid. The Fourth Crusade, which ended with the sacking of Constantinople, destroyed the Byzantine Empire and opened the door for the Muslim Turks to expand farther westward. Not only did the Crusades fail in their purpose, but from Europe's point of view they also made matters worse.

From another perspective, though, the Crusades were successful at least in stemming the Islamic invasion of Europe. After the founding of Islam in the seventh century, it spread throughout the Mediterranean region (see "The Spread of Islam" in Chapter 1). Sardinia, Corsica, Sicily, parts of southern Italy, North Africa, and much of Spain fell to Muslim invaders. From Spain, Muslims launched an invasion of France in the eighth century, though that invasion was beaten back. In the early 1000s Muslims advanced on Rome, but with similar results. During the Crusades and after, Spain reclaimed its territory in what was called the Reconquista (see "Spanish Islam" in Chapter 1), which ended when the Spanish monarchy raised its flag over Granada in 1492. Historians can only speculate, but it seems likely that without the Crusades, Islam would have made further inroads into Europe.

One important outcome of the Crusades is that they diminished the power of the popes and increased the power of Europe's monarchs. It was King Ferdinand and Queen Isabella, not a pope, who drove the Muslims out of Spain (and who financed Columbus's expedition). After the Roman Empire broke apart in the fifth century, western Europe was in a state of chaos. Bandits and warlike tribes overran much of the continent. No one seemed to have the power to drive them away. Feudalism emerged as a social and economic structure that provided people some measure of protection against violence and invasion (see "The Structure of Medieval Society" in Chapter 9).

Feudalism also had the effect of breaking Europe into small, competing principalities (the territories of princes), duchies (the territories of dukes), and feudal estates. While a king, in theory, ruled over a kingdom such as France or England, real power was in the hands of dukes, counts, and barons who ruled regions of the country. In turn, these regions were divided into smaller landholdings governed by the nobles' vassals, that is, those men who had sworn oaths of loyalty to the nobles in exchange for protection; these men, in turn, frequently made grants of land to knights. This structure is reflected in the names of many of the important Crusaders: Godfrey of Bouillon, Hugh of Vermandois, Raymond of Toulouse. These men were not "French." Rather, they identified themselves with a region of France or even a city.

This patchwork of small regions created a power vacuum that was filled by the Catholic Church and the pope. The concept of Christendom imposed some sort of common purpose over the fragmented states of Europe. Many popes, seeing themselves as Europe's true "kings," wanted to expand their authority. Urban II, for example, called the First Crusade in 1095 in large part to extend the power of the Catholic Church, perhaps even to force the Eastern Orthodox Church, another branch of Christianity in the East, to submit to him (see "Religious Separation of East and West" in Chapter 1). Pope Innocent III, who called the Fourth Crusade in 1199, believed that the pope was the supreme monarch on earth, not just of the church, but of the state as well. He became obsessed with recapturing Jerusalem not because Jerusalem was the site of Christ's tomb, but mainly because it was not part of his worldly "empire."

The failure of the later Crusades to recapture Jerusalem began to break the backs of the popes. After the First Crusade, kings were leading the Crusades: Louis VII of France (Second Crusade), Richard I of England and Philip II of France (Third Crusade), Holy Roman Emperor Frederick II (Sixth Crusade), and Louis IX of France (Seventh Crusade). In effect, Europe's kings were competing with the pope for power. The best example is the Sixth Crusade, which Frederick II—who defied the authority of the pope—conducted without authorization from Rome. The pope, Gregory VII, was so determined to hold back the ambitious Frederick that he made preparations to invade Frederick's realms in Italy while the emperor was on this Crusade. Ten years later Gregory called a Crusade not against "the infidels" (unbelievers, referring to Muslims), but against

Frederick, one of Europe's Christian kings. Frederick fought back and ignored the pope when he excommunicated, or expelled, Frederick from the church.

As Europe's kings were beginning to assert themselves, that is, to claim power and authority, the Crusades were transforming the feudal makeup of Europe. So many of the old feudal lords had either died in the Crusades or transplanted themselves and their families to Palestine and Syria that power began to shift upward toward the king. Now, people were not just citizens of, say, Aquitaine or Toulouse. They were beginning to think of themselves as French. Similar changes took place in England, Italy, and the Holy Roman Empire.

In time, this shift of power from the pope to temporal (worldly) rulers would allow more democratic forms of government to emerge. Even during the Crusades, this process began to take place in England with the Magna Carta, or "Great Charter." The Magna Carta does not make very interesting reading in the twenty-first century, however. It consists of sixty-three demands the nobles of England made of King John I in 1215. They all had to do with such issues as taxes and inheritance laws. The point of the Magna Carta is that it exists, that the English barons made and won their demands. It was the first step toward a more constitutional form of government. Power was flowing from the pope and the church to civil rulers, such as kings and queens. From there it was beginning to flow downward to the people, although this process would take centuries more to complete.

Columbus launches his voyage to the New World

Columbus's goal in sailing to the Far East in part was to establish a base from which Christians could launch a new Crusade to the Middle East. In his journal, dated December 26, 1492, he said that he wanted all the profits from his voyage to be used to finance the conquest of Jerusalem. In his will, he created a fund that he directed to be used for a Crusade.

While Columbus's dream was never realized, his voyages marked the beginning of a new Europe, one that was

A brass celestial globe from thirteenth-century Arabia. Without the advances in astronomy such as this, Columbus, as well as numerous other European explorers, would have lacked the navigational tools needed to make his voyage. *Copyright The British Museum. Reproduced by permission.*

very different from the Europe of 1095 when Pope Urban II had called the First Crusade. Many of the changes in Europe resulted from the Crusades. At the beginning of the Crusades, Europe was almost barbaric. The major European cities—London, Paris, and Rome—were backward places compared with cities in the East. There, civilization flourished, not only in the Byzantine Empire (the seat of the Eastern Orthodox Church) but also in such great cities as Thebes, Memphis,

Nineveh, Tyre, Sidon, Damascus, Baghdad, and Jerusalem. In these cities, learning was far more advanced than it was in Europe. They were home to libraries (Damascus alone had seventy libraries) and museums; to advances in medicine and science; to astronomers, mathematicians, skilled crafts workers, and engineers.

Crusaders returned to Europe with new ideas, new foods, and even new words. Alchemy, alcohol, alcove, algebra, algorithm, alkali, amalgam, and arsenal are just some of the "a" words that came from the Middle East. Other borrowings, both of concepts and words, include bazaar, benzene, borax, camphor, cipher, elixir, sequin, soda, talisman, tariff, zenith, and many more from the work of Arab scientists, geographers, poets, and astronomers.

Without the advances in astronomy that came from Arabia, for example, Columbus—as well as numerous other explorers from Spain, Portugal, and Italy—would have lacked the navigational tools needed to make his voyage. The astrolabe, for instance, was a device used for navigation and timekeeping at sea by plotting the positions of the sun and stars (whose names Europe also adopted from the Arabs). The astrolabe was widely used in the Islamic world by 800 and was introduced to Europe by Muslims in Spain early in the twelfth century. Columbus also would have used a navigational tool called a quadrant, which measured altitude and was developed from the Arabs' *kamal*.

The list of products that Europe acquired from the Middle East seems almost endless. There were fruits—such as limes, lemons, apricots, and oranges—and spices, such as nutmeg, cinnamon, caraway, tarragon, and saffron. Fabrics included damask, satin, silk, and mohair, as well as exotic oriental carpets and the dyes used to color these fabrics. The Crusades led to increased European demand for fine silver and gold jewelry, articles made of precious stones, glassware, and tools made of hard Damascus steel, all from the Middle East and other parts of the world. Among the musical instruments taken back to Europe were the shawm (a woodwind instrument), the lute, and various kinds of drums.

Meanwhile, the Crusades encouraged other important changes in Europe. New roads were built to accommodate pilgrims traveling to the Holy Land. Warfare, as it always

A leaf from the Koran, the Muslim holy book, written in Arabic script. To better understand Islam, clerics often translated Arabic philosophical texts, including the Koran. ©*Werner Forman/Art Resource, NY. Reproduced by permission.*

does, introduced new forms of technology, including more effective weapons, and new architectural techniques learned from building better castles. Novel ways of paying for the ventures led to the development of trade, commerce, shipbuilding, finance, and credit around the Mediterranean. New forms of taxation to fund the later Crusades led to the development of more modern systems for collecting and distributing revenues for public ventures. It also became easier for Europe to keep track of this money. In about 1202 Europe abandoned Roman numerals in favor of what are still called Arabic numerals.

The key point is that westerners were becoming more aware of the wider world. They translated numerous Arabic texts, including medical, mathematical, and scientific books and books on such fields as optics and magnetism. They established universities that were starting to put this knowledge to use, much of it collected by western scholars who had traveled to the East to study. To better understand Islam (usually, though, with the goal of converting Muslims to Christianity), clerics (clergymen) translated Arabic philosophical texts, and Abbot Peter the Venerable even translated the Koran, the Muslim holy book. Schools were set up in Europe to teach eastern languages, and many missionaries traveled throughout the Middle East and Far East trying to win converts. They returned to Europe with geographical knowledge that expanded the world for Europeans. Europe was emerging from its Dark Ages and from under the thumb of the pope, and many of the fruits of the Crusades created a climate of exploration and curiosity that enabled Columbus and others to gain funding for their voyages.

The Jews are expelled from Spain

The Crusades drove a permanent wedge between Islam and the West. For centuries after Jerusalem fell to the Muslims in 638, Muslims and Christians lived side by side in relative harmony. Some historians believe that during the centuries between 638 and the First Crusade, more Christians than Muslims lived in the Middle East. Numerous Christian sects, or subgroups, flourished, including groups with such names as the Jacobites in Syria, the Copts in Egypt, and the Nestorians of Persia. Each of these groups had its own history, its own interpretation of the Christian message, its own churches, and its own vital community. Many of these Christians held high offices alongside Muslims.

The Crusades, of course, changed that. After Acre fell, Christians in the Middle East began to retreat. Many were fearful of the victorious Muslims and converted to Islam. The Mongols who invaded the region in the thirteenth century came to believe that Allah, the God of Islam, was the true God, so they, too, converted to Islam. Put simply, Islam won the Crusades, at least from one perspective. They drove out the Christians, converted the Mongols, and turned the Byzantine Empire into the Muslim Ottoman Empire, which survived in Asia Minor and surrounding regions until the twentieth century.

In the view of many historians, the Crusades have still not ended. They point out that the same tensions persist in the Middle East that existed a thousand years ago. Pales-

Palestinian children show off their weapons, catapults and slingshots, which originated during the Crusades. Even after the Crusades, as well as numerous other conflicts throughout the centuries, the Middle East continues to be entangled in turmoil.
© Alain Nogues/Corbis Sygma. Reproduced by permission.

tine became part of the Turkish Ottoman Empire, but in the peace that was declared after World War I (1914–18), it came under British control. Finally, in 1948, the Jewish nation of Israel was formed out of Palestine. The Jews, after having been driven out of so many places, from Old Testament times until 1492 Spain and beyond, now had a homeland that included the city of the Temple of Solomon, Jerusalem (see "Judaism" in Chapter 1).

A glance at the headlines of any current newspaper on any given day shows that peace still has not come to this troubled region. Jewish Israel is surrounded by Muslim nations that see Israel as hostile occupiers of their holy land. Israel relies heavily on military aid from its chief ally, the United States, which has a long-standing cultural connection with the Jews. The first settlers in America were the Pilgrims, a reminder of the pilgrimages to the Holy Land in the Middle Ages (roughly 500–1500). The first Pilgrims gave many of their towns Old Testament names, such as Hebron, Salem,

Bethlehem, Zion, and Judea. Despite some anti-Semitism (anti-Jewish prejudice), many Jews have found a home in the United States and live in relative peace.

In contrast, Jews in Israel feel as though they are under a constant state of siege against the Arab Muslim nations that surround the country, as do Muslim Palestinians in territories occupied by the Israelis. The result is constant violence and terrorism. The focus of much of the violence is the United States, which is often seen in the Middle East as a new Crusader force, ignorant of Islam and deeply prejudiced against Muslims. To some observers, it was unfortunate that President George W. Bush used the word *crusade* in discussing the war against terrorism after the September 11, 2001, attacks on America. Such a word could suggest to the Muslim world a repeat of historical events now nearly a millennium old. The president's supporters, however, noted that the "crusade" was against terrorism, not Islam.

Meanwhile, the crushed remains of Crusader castles dot the landscape in Palestine. And as Franklin Hamilton notes in his book *The Crusades:* "History may never repeat itself, but certain patterns seem eternal, and the struggle for that sun-parched scrap of earth known as the Holy Land is still going on, in the atomic age as in the days of mounted knights."

For More Information

Books

Brundage, James A. *The Crusades: A Documentary Survey.* Milwaukee, WI: Marquette University Press, 1962.

Chamber, Mortimer, et al. *The Western Experience.* 8th ed. Boston: McGraw-Hill, 2003.

Erbstösser, Martin. *The Crusades.* Translated by C. S. V. Salt. New York: Universe Books, 1979.

Hamilton, Franklin. *The Crusades.* New York: Dial Press, 1965.

Prawer, Joshua. *The World of the Crusaders.* New York: Quadrangle Books, 1972.

Saunders, J. J. *Aspects of the Crusades.* Christchurch, New Zealand: Whitcomb and Tombs, 1969.

Index

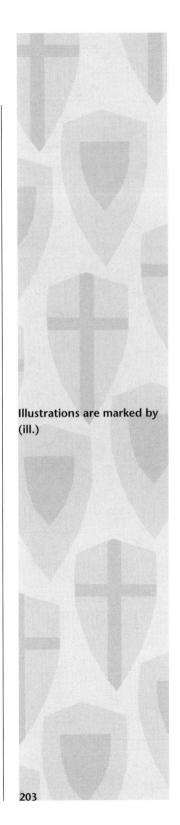

Illustrations are marked by (ill.)

O

Odovacar 7
Otto I 10

P

Palestinian children 200 (ill.)
Parzival 179
Paula of Bethlehem, Saint 46
Pelagius, Cardinal 108–09
Penance 36–37
People's Crusade 54–56
Pepin the Short 8
Percival; or, The Story of the Grail
    178 (ill.)
Peter the Hermit 54–55, 132 (ill.)
Philip II 96–99, 158 (ill.)
Philip IV 154
Pilgrimages 33–46
Primogeniture 60

Q

Qalawun, al-Mansur 189–90
Qutuz, Saif al-Din 186–88

R

Ramleh 41–42
Raymond of Toulouse 76, 85–86
Reynald of Châtillon 95
Richard I (Lionheart) 59, 60 (ill.),
    66, 96–101, 123 (ill.), 124
Richard II, Duke of Normandy 35
Ridwan 79
Romance 175–80
Roman Empire 2, 5–7, 10
Romanus IV Diogenes 49

S

Saladin 28, 66, 94, 96–101, 123
    (ill.), 124
Saladin tithe 98
Second Crusade 90–94
Second Temple 5–6

Seljuks 48–52, 71, 75, 116,
    119–21, 120 (ill.)
Seventh Crusade 113–14, 183–84
Shahnameh 169 (ill.)
Shiite Muslims 72, 116, 119–20
Sir Gawain and the Green Knight 178
Sixth Crusade 10, 110–13, 194–95
Song of Roland, The 172 (ill.) *See
    also Chason de Roland*
Sunni Muslims 72, 75, 77, 116, 119

T

Tancred 61
Temple of Solomon 5, 14
Teutonic Knights 155
Theodosius I 6–7
Third Crusade 10, 95–101
Tomb of the Mamluks 186 (ill.)
Tomb of the Virgin 45
Treaty of Jaffa 28, 112–13
Tripoli, taking of 77 (ill.)
Troubadours 174
Trouvères 174
True Cross 27 (ill.), 28, 42, 44
    (ill.), 108, 127 (ill.)
Tunisia 75 (ill.)

U

Umar 17, 23
Umayyads 72
Urban II, Pope 1, 52, 53 (ill.), 59,
    83–84, 142
Urfa 62 (ill.)
Uthman 72

V

Via Dolorosa 42
Violence 139–40

W

Warfare 157–67
    weapons used during 159 (ill.),
    163 (ill.), 165 (ill.)

William, Duke of Normandy 9
William of Rubruck 183
Women Crusaders 36

DATE DUE

MAR 3 1 2022			
			PRINTED IN U.S.A.